Eric Newby was born in London in 1919 and was
educated at St Paul's School. In 1938 he joined the
four-masted Finnish barque *Moshulu* as an apprentice
and sailed in the last Grain Race from Australia to Europe
by way of Cape Horn. During the Second World War
he served in the Black Watch and Special Boat Section,
and was a prisoner-of-war from 1942 to 1945. After the war
his world expanded still further – into the fashion business
and book publishing. Whatever else he was doing, he always
travelled on a grand scale, either under his own steam
or as Travel Editor of the *Observer.*

Mr Newby's other books include *The Last Grain Race,*
Slowly Down the Ganges, Love and War in the Apennines,
The Big Red Train Ride, A Short Walk in the Hindu Kush,
On the Shores of the Mediterranean, Round Ireland
in Low Gear, an anthology, *A Traveller's Life, A Book*
of Traveller's Tales and *A Small Place in Italy,*
all of which are available in Picador.

Also by Eric Newby
in Picador

A Short Walk in the Hindu Kush
Slowly Down the Ganges
Love and War in the Apennines
A Book of Travellers' Tales
On the Shores of the Mediterranean
Round Ireland in Low Gear
The Big Red Train Ride
The Last Grain Race
A Traveller's Life
A Small Place in Italy

ERIC NEWBY

SOMETHING WHOLESALE

My Life and Times in the Rag Trade

PICADOR

First published 1962 by Martin Secker and Warburg Ltd
Revised edition published 1970 by Hodder and Stoughton Ltd

This edition published 1985 by Picador
an imprint of Macmillan General Books
25 Eccleston Place London SW1W 9NF
and Basingstoke

Associated companies throughout the world

ISBN 0 330 28778 8

12 14 16 18 19 17 15 13

A CIP catalogue record for this book is available
from the British Library

Printed and bound in Great Britain by
Cox & Wyman Ltd, Reading, Berkshire

To My Father
Splendid in Defeat

ACKNOWLEDGEMENTS

I would like to thank Beatrix
Miller, Editor of British *Vogue* for her
kindness in allowing me to go to Paris
with her fashion team, to attend the
showings of the 1985 Spring/
Summer Haute Couture Collections.
And I would also like to thank
Felicity Clark and Elizabeth Tibaris
of *Vogue* for putting up with me while
I was there.

CONTENTS

PREFACE

THE HERO of this book, if it has one, is the man who, during the years it describes, was head of the dressmaking firm of Lane and Newby—in other words my father. But this was my father in old age. We were separated by a great gulf of years, and when I was old enough to appreciate him the world which he knew and of which he was a part had passed away.

What do I know of my father as a young man? Practically nothing. His father came from the East Riding of Yorkshire and he acquired a stepmother at an early age. I know that with her his life was not very happy. It was one of the few things that when he spoke of it moved him to tears.

I look at photographs of him in our family albums taken when he was twenty or so—great group photographs of men and girls upriver, perhaps, after an outing or a regatta —and wonder what he and his companions were really like. He was very handsome, this is obvious—with a fine, well-tended moustache—and he was elegant, either in a negligent manner with a silk handkerchief knotted round his neck and a panama hat with the brim turned up in the front or else more formally in a dark suit with a watch chain and a straw hat with a black band.

The girls are dressed to the nines with fichus of lace and hats like great presentation baskets of fruit from Fortnums.

They must be upriver. In the background of the particular picture of which I am thinking there is a white clap-boarded house. It is probably a club-house or it might be a mill and beyond it the woods are thick and green, like the Quarry Woods at Marlow, only the house is not at Marlow.

11

Where is it? I wish I knew. There is no one left to ask. Perhaps, somewhere, one or two of those young men and women are left alive, but they would be very old now.

Some of the girls must have been beautiful but one must make an effort of will to believe it. Their clothes makes them seem older than they really were. And the way in which the photographer took his pictures endows them with too much chin, or else no chin at all. They look absurdly young or else like maiden aunts. The effort of keeping still for the photographer on that warm summer's day and looking into the sun was too much for them, particularly for the men. Some of them are squinting, some are out of focus, some have an air of being slightly insane. It is gratifying to see that in all these groups my father took the precaution of seating himself next to the most good-looking girl available. I would like to know how they spoke, these friends of my father; the idioms they used; the things that made them laugh; but I shall never know, more's the pity and neither will my children.

There are more rural scenes. Photographs taken not by a professional but by one of my father's companions when they were camping, in the doorway of a tent, early in the morning with the mist still rising from the meadows. They look dishevelled, as if none of them had slept well, perhaps there were horses in the field. One of them is smoking a meerschaum pipe with a Turk's head carved on it. In the foreground there is a large black cooking pot, suspended from a metal tripod, simmering over a wood fire. All the cooking equipment is tremendously heavy. How did they get it there? They must have used a horse-drawn vehicle. It is a pity that there is no picture of it.

There is a series of photographs taken off the East Coast in a yacht with a hired man. "He was a real old salt," my father told me. In these pictures he and his friends are all wearing black and white striped trousers rolled up to the knees and stockinette caps. In the background of one of them there is a light-ship and close to it a barquentine, deep-loaded, running before the wind. Whoever took the photograph had difficulty with it because the horizon goes rapidly downhill! "There was a bit of a lop on," my father said, wistfully. He had always wanted to be a sailor. And when his father married again he tried to run away to sea but was brought back in a cab. Next in time are the photographs of my mother taken the year before I was born, looking gentle and rather sad, and another of my father looking severe and bristly reclining on a velvet cushion up in the bows of his skiff. I wonder how things went that day. Was she having sculling lessons at that time? Perhaps she wasn't getting her hands away properly.

The next photographs are of my father partially domesticated, taken on the beach at Frinton. I am on the scene now, large and shiny in a large, shiny pram. I look like an advertisement for some health food. I think my father has just arrived from London on the afternoon train. He is dressed for London. Looking at the photograph now I almost convince myself that I remember the moment when it was taken. But who took it? I seem to remember a nurse with starched cuffs and dark rings under her eyes who used to have assignations with old men in the local cemetery when she was supposed to be giving me an airing, and was summarily fired for it. Perhaps she took the picture.

There are pictures on Sark. I am sitting on my father's head as he wades through the bracken. It was an enchanting spot in the Twenties. There are a lot of photographs of the Twenties. My mother in a cloche hat at Deauville. Scenes at Branscombe in Devonshire of two sisters, both store buyers, Lolly and Polly, friends of my parents, identical in long jerseys and strings of beads, surrounded by a whole pack of Pekinese.

Lolly was the best suit buyer in London. She was extremely

good-hearted but could be extremely autocratic. On one occasion a customer had a suit on approval and, thinking that she would not be detected, wore it at the Royal Military Meeting at Sandown Park, where she was seen by Lolly, who was mad about racing.

On the following Monday the customer returned to the store and complained that the suit which she was wearing had some imperfection in it and demanded a reduction in price.

"If there's something wrong with it," said Lolly, "then you shan't bloody well have it."

She made her take it off in a fitting-room. "Now bloody well go home without it!" she said.

Eventually the customer had to buy another suit in order to leave the building, one that was even more expensive than the original, which Lolly promptly marked-down in price and appropriated to her own use, having wanted it for herself in the first place.

There is a whole gallery of memorable characters in these albums. Captain and Mrs. Buckle—Mrs. Buckle smoked a hundred cigarettes a day. "Gaspers" she used to call them, and her voice was reduced to a hollow croak. Ivor—a young man who had an open Vauxhall with a boat-shaped body and used to drive to Devonshire in silk pyjamas after parties in London. He inherited a fortune when he was twenty-one, got through it in a year and became a bus driver. He used to wave to my mother when he drove the number nines over Hammersmith Bridge. And there is another buyer called Phyll— who lived in sin with someone called Uncle Fred, who wasn't an uncle. At Christmas time Auntie Phyll's flat resembled a robber's cave with presents from manufacturers piled high in it. Those were days when a fashion buyer was expected to feather her nest (nobody else was going to do it for her) and many a buyer was able to retire to a riverside cottage on the proceeds of the toll she exacted from the manufacturers on every dress that went into her department. On one occasion a disgruntled manufacturer informed the management that Auntie Phyll was taking a percentage in this way but was nonplussed when he was told by the Managing Director that they didn't care what bribes she received providing that the clothes she bought were as well chosen and as cheap as those of their competitors.

And there is a whole supporting cast of rural characters from the village where we had taken a cottage for the summer. Photographs of the innkeeper, who was having a violent affair with the barmaid under the nose of his wife; photographs of *his* wife and the barmaid, who looks very innocent in a velvet dress, and pictures of village children with whom I used to float paper boats down an open sewer; and the policeman's son who taught me to say bloody. Once for a bet I drank the water from the sewer. The results were not what normal medical experience would lead one to expect. Instead of contracting dysentery I had a complete stoppage of the bowels that lasted for more than a week.

And there is the last photograph I have of my father. He is sitting with my mother in an umpire's launch on the river at Hammersmith. It is the summer of the year he died. He has shrunk with the years, but with his white club cap he looks for all the world like a mischievous schoolboy.

CHAPTER ONE

A SHORT HISTORY OF
THE SECOND WORLD WAR

ONE MORNING in August 1940 " A " Company, Infantry Wing, was on parade outside the Old Buildings at the Royal Military College, Camberley. Company Sergeant-Major Clegg, a foxy looking Grenadier, was addressing us ". . . THERE WILL BE NO WEEK-END LEAF," he screamed with satisfaction. (There never had been.) "That means no women for Mr. Pont, Mr. Pont (there were two Mr. Ponts—cousins). Take that smile off your face Mr. Newby or you'll be inside. Wiring and Demolition Practice at 1100 hours is cancelled for Number One Platoon. Instead there will be Bridging Practice. Bridging Equipment will be drawn at 1030 hours. CUMPNEE . . . CUMPNEEEE . . . SHAAH! "

"Heaven," said the Ponts as we doubled smartly to our rooms to change for P.T. "There's nothing more ghastly than all that wire."

I, too, was glad that there was to be no Wiring and Demolition. Both took place in a damp, dark wood. Wiring was hell at any rate and Demolition for some mysterious reason was conducted by a civilian. It always seemed to me the last thing a civilian should have a hand in and I was not surprised when, later in the war, he disappeared in a puff of smoke, hoist by one of his own petards.

In June 1940, after six months of happy oblivion as a private soldier, I had been sent to Sandhurst to be converted into an officer.

Pressure of events had forced the Royal Military College to convert itself into an O.C.T.U., an Officer Cadet Training Unit, and the permanent staff still referred meaningfully in the presence of the new intakes to a golden age "when the gennulmen cadets were 'ere".

"Ere" we learned to drill in an impressive fashion and our ability to command was strengthened by the Adjutant, magnificent in breeches and riding boots from Maxwell, who had us stationed in pairs on the closely mown lawns that sloped gently to the lake. A quarter of a mile apart, he made us screech at one another, marching and countermarching imaginary battalions by the left, by the right and by the centre until our voices broke under the strain and whirred away into nothingness.

Less well we carried out a drill with enormous military bicycles as complex as the evolutions performed by Lippizanas at the Spanish Riding School. On these treadmills which each weighed between sixty and seventy pounds, we used to wobble off into the surrounding pine plantations, which we shared uneasily with working parties of lunatics from the asylum at Broadmoor, for T.E.W.T.s—Tactical Exercises Without Troops.

Whether moving backwards or forwards the T.E.W.T. world was a strange, isolated one in which the lunatics who used to wave to us as we laid down imaginary fields of fire against an imaginary enemy might have been equally at home. In it aircraft were rarely mentioned, tanks never. We were members of the Infantry Wing. There was an Armoured Wing for those who were interested in such things as tanks and armoured cars and the authorities had no intention of allowing the two departments to mingle. Gradually we succumbed to the pervasive unreality.

"I want to bring home to you the meaning of this war," said a visiting General. "In four months those of you who are not R.T.U.'d—Returned to your Units—will be platoon commanders. In six months time most of you will be dead."

And we believed him. Our numbers were already depleted by a mysterious outbreak of bed-wetting—an R.T.U.-able offence. In a military trance we imagined ourselves waving ashplants, charging machine-gun nests at the head of our men. The Carrara marble pillars, which supported the roof of the chapel in which we carried out our militant devotions, were scarcely sufficient to contain the names of all those other "gennulmen" who, in the earlier war, had died in the mud at Passchendaele and among the wire on the forward slopes of the Hohenzollern Redoubt. They had sat where we were sitting and their names were set out in neat columns on the pillars like debit entries in some terrible ledger.

This dream of Death or Glory affected our leisure. Most of us had passed our formative years in the outer suburbs. Now, to make ourselves more acceptable to our employers we took up beagling (the College had the Eton Beagles for the duration); ordered shirts we couldn't afford from expensive shirtmakers in Jermyn Street and drank Black Velvet in the Hotel. The snugger pubs were out of bounds for fear we might meet a barmaid who "did it". No one but a maniac would have wanted to do it with the one at the Hotel.

The bridging equipment was housed in a low, sinister-looking shed near the lake on which we were to practise. This was not the ornamental lake in front of the Old Buildings on which, in peace time, playful cadets used to float chamber pots containing lighted candles—a practice now forbidden by the blackout regulations. It was an inferior lake, little more than a pond; from it rose a dank smell of rotting vegetation.

Inside the shed there were a number of small decked-in pontoons and strips of heavy teak grating which were intended to form the footway. Blocks and tackle hung in great swathes from the roof; presumably they were to hold the bridge steady in a swiftly flowing stream. Everything seemed unnecessarily heavy, as though it was part of the gear of a wooden ship-of-the-line.

There was every sign that the bridge had not been used for years—if at all. The custodian, a grumpy old pensioner rooted out of his cottage to open the door, confirmed this.

"What yer think yer going to do with it, cross the Channel?" he croaked.

The Staff Sergeant detailed to instruct us in the use of the bridge was uneasy. He had never seen anything like it before. It bore no resemblance to any kind of bridge that he had encountered.

"It's not an ISSUE BRIDGE," he kept repeating, plaintively. "Gennulmen, you *must* help me." We were deaf to him. The Army had seldom been kind to us; it was too late to call us gentlemen.

Finally, after rooting in the darkness he discovered a battered manual hanging on a nail behind the door. It confirmed our suspicions that the bridge had been constructed at the time of the Boer War. No surprise at the Royal Military College where a whole literature of the same period—text books filled with drawings of blockhouses with corrugated-iron roofs; men with droopy moustaches peering through loopholes; and armoured trains that I associated with the early life of Mr. Winston Churchill—were piled high on the tops of cupboards in the lecture rooms and had obviously only recently fallen into disuse.

With the manual in his hand the Sergeant was once more on familiar ground—if one can use such an expression in connection with a bridge. His spirits rose still further when he discovered that there was a drill laid down for assembling the monstrous thing.

"On the command 'One' the even numbers of the front ranks will about turn, grasp the Caissons with both hands and advance into the water. On the command 'Two' the odd numbers of the front rank will peg out the Guys, Retaining Caisson. On the command 'Three' the even numbers of the rear rank will pick up the Sections, Decking" . . . and so on.

On the command "One" the Caisson Party, of which I was one, moved gingerly into the water, which was surprisingly warm. Some of the more frivolous cadets began to splash one another, but were rebuked by the Sergeant. After some twenty minutes all the Caissons were in position, secured by block and tackle.

"Caisson Party, about turn, quick march!" To the accompaniment of weird sucking noises we squelched ashore.

"Decking Party, advance!" The Decking Party staggered forward under its appalling load. Standing on the bank, with the water streaming from the bottoms of our trousers, we watched them go.

"It all seems rather pointless when we've already walked across," someone said.

"Quiet!" said the Sergeant. "The next cadet who speaks goes on a charge." He was looking at his watch, apprehensively.

"Decking Party and Caisson Party will retire and unpile arms," he went on. We had already performed the complicated operation of piling arms. It was one of the things we really knew how to do. "Now then, get a move on."

We had just completed the unpiling when Sergeant-Major Clegg appeared on the far side of the lake, stiff as a ramrod, jerkily propelling one of our gigantic bicycles. Dismounted, standing half-hidden in the undergrowth, he looked more foxy than ever.

He addressed us and the world in that high-pitched sustained scream that even now, when I recall it at dead of night twenty years later, makes me come to attention even when lying in my bed.

"SAAAAN ALUN!"

"SAAAAH!"

"DOZEEEE . . . DOZEEEE . . . GET THOSE DOZY, IDUL GENNULMEN OVER THE BRIDGE . . . AT . . . THER . . . DUBBOOOOL!"

"SAAAAH!" shrieked Sergeant Allen and wheeled upon us with a face bereft of all humanity. "PLATOOOON, PLATOOOON WILL CROSS THE BRIDGE AT THER DUBOOL—DUBOOOOL!"

Armed to the teeth, bowed down by gas masks, capes antigas, token anti-tank rifles and 2" mortars made of wood (all the real ones had been taken away from us after Dunkirk), we thundered down the bank and on to the bridge.

The weight of thirty men was too much for it; there was a noise like a succession of pistol shots as the Guys, Retaining Caisson parted, the central span of the bridge surged away and the whole body of us crashed into the water. It was like the end of the Gadarene Swine, the Tay Bridge Disaster and the Crossing of the Beresina reproduced in miniature.

As we came to the surface, ornamented with weed and surrounded by the token wooden weapons which, surprisingly, in spite of their weight, floated, we began to laugh hysterically and what had begun as a military operation ended as a water frolic. The caissons became rafts on which were spread-eagled the waterlogged figures of what had until recently been officer cadets, who now resembled nothing more than a band of lascivious Tritons. People were ducking one another; the Ponts were floating calmly, contemplating the sky as if off-shore at noon at Eden Roc . . .

Gradually the laughter ceased and a terrible silence descended on us. A tall ascetic figure was looking down on us with a mixture of incredulity and disgust from an ornamental bridge in the rustic taste. The Sergeant was saluting furiously; Sergeant-Major Clegg, foxy to the last, had slipped away into the undergrowth—only his bicycle, propped against a tree, showed that he had ever been there. The face on the bridge was a very well-known face.

Without a word General de Gaulle turned on his heel and went off, followed by a train of officers of high rank. His visit had been unannounced at his special request so that he could see us working under natural conditions. What he must have thought is unimaginable. France had just fallen. It must have confirmed his worst suspicions of the British Army. Perhaps the intransigence that was later to become a characteristic was born there on that bright morning beside a steamy little lake in Surrey.

For Sergeant Allen the morning's work had a more immediate significance. His career seemed blasted.

"You've gone and done me in," he said sadly, as we fell in to squelch back to the Old Buildings.

Four years, seven months and twenty-five days after that first abortive amphibious operation amongst the Camberley pines I stood on the dockside at Tilbury, the last of the last boatload of returning prisoners from Oflag 79.

I was much changed since that far-off day when Company

Sergeant-Major Clegg had told me to take that smile off my face. Then, at least, I had been a soldier in embryo. Now, wearing a suit of battle dress that had been made for a giant, sprinkled liberally with delousing powder, which the authorities at Brussels had thought necessary before allowing me out to eat an ersatz gooseberry tart on Boulevard Anspach, I resembled nothing human, civil or military.

En masse, my companions and I were not objects of compassion. Ten days of liberty during which we had roamed the countryside of Saxony, searching for food that the local farmers had been too terrified to withhold from us, had so inflated our faces that they resembled grotesque balloons at a carnival, in startling contrast with our emaciated bodies, which were concealed by our uniforms.

Unlike the returned prisoner of popular imagination we were heavily laden: with kitbags stuffed with coats and great rubber riding mackintoshes bought at officers shops along the route, and with long woollen underpants that had been pressed upon us by helping organisations. In addition I was encumbered with a number of scientific instruments which I had looted from a German experimental station, under the impression that they would make my fortune, and, heaviest of all to bear, an anxiety neurosis brought on by my failure to complete, before liberation, a petit-point fire screen, one of thousands sent out by the Red Cross with the express purpose of allaying anxiety neurosis. I still have the instruments. No one has ever been able to tell me what they are intended for. I burned the fire screen and felt better for having done so.

It began to rain heavily. "Officers this way," said a sergeant from the disembarkation staff and we trailed after him under the arc lights, across greasy railway tracks on which tank engines hissed with steam up, to a long, low, wooden hut. Inside the other ranks were already eating bacon and eggs and drinking tea which was being served to them by cheerful, common ATS.

We were given tea by members of a more fashionable volunteer organisation whose roots were deep in S.W.7. They seemed more interested in the effect that they were producing on a number of men, who had not seen an English woman for anything up to five years, than in producing the victuals for which we still craved.

"Do you know Jamie Stuart Ogilvie-Keir-Gordon in the Scots Guards? I think he was with you."

"No, I'm afraid not."

"Or Binkie Martyn-Sikes? "

"No! "

"How very odd that you shouldn't have known *him*. He's my second cousin."

"Do you think it would be possible for me to have something to eat? "

"Oh, how stupid of me. It's been so interesting talking to you I quite forgot."

Whilst we were eating a Colonel entered. He was large, with a face as red as the tabs on his lapels.

"Carry on, gentlemen," he said, genially. No one had in fact stopped. His costume was an unconvincing parody of a panoply which I now associated with a long-dead past. Neither breeches nor boots were as those worn by the terrifying but beautiful Eddie, our Adjutant at Sandhurst. Particularly the boots; they were down-at-heel as though they had been worn over-much on urban pavements.

He sat himself down on the edge of one of the tables and tapped his awful boots with a little swagger cane.

"Before you chaps move on from here," he said with a bonhomie which we found extremely distasteful, "there is just one thing I would like to say to you.

"We realise here that things have been pretty rough for you on the other side. The Hun's finished, now it's our turn. I expect you saw some pretty rotten things—atrocities. I happen to be the Commandant of a P.O.W. Camp at —— (he named a place somewhere remote in East Anglia) I'm also," he added, surprisingly, "a Member of Parliament. If you've witnessed any kind of atrocity in the last few years I would like you to report it to me, now. I promise you that whatever you tell me here will be brought home to the men in my camp. They'll sweat it out."

It had been a long day. I thought of the journey we had made through Belgium. There had been a shortage of rolling stock and we had entrained in carriages intended for the transportation of German prisoners. The windows were festooned with barbed wire. At the halts, which were numerous, small boys had thrown stones at us under the impression that we were members of the opposition. Who was to blame them? I thought of Germany—how I loathed pine trees and Alsatian dogs. I thought of the camp near Munich: the S.S. stripping Yugoslav men and women, kicking them round the compound in the snow and later singing harmoniously together in their huts, full of *gemütlichkeit*. I had seen a lot of things and this was too much.

Finally, an officer, who had been captured with the Rifle Brigade at Calais in 1940, got to his feet.

"Colonel," he said, "I have two observations to make. The first is that you yourself are, without doubt, the biggest atrocity I have seen in the last five years. Secondly, the sooner there is a by-election in your constituency the better.

"And in case," he went on, "you are now thinking of having me placed under arrest I will tell you that I have not yet been medically examined and I am probably quite insane

—and that, Colonel, goes for everyone else in this room."

There was a long, long train journey from Tilbury to Sussex without changing—a tour-de-force only possible in time of total war; the train stopping in the small hours of the morning at a disused platform deep in the bowels of Holborn viaduct.

"Hasn't been used since 1918," said the guard. He stood on the platform ankle deep in black soot, the accumulation of twenty-seven years, whilst those of us who lived in London argued whether or not to abandon the train and take taxis.

"Can't get a taxi in London after midnight—Yanks," said a gloomy looking Major with a handlebar moustache and little tufts of ginger hair growing out of his cheeks. "Had a letter from m'brother." At dawn the train crept into Barnes Station. I lived at Hammersmith Bridge, five minutes away by bus. It seemed ridiculous not to get out. I started assembling my extraordinary luggage. "Chap told me at Tilbury," the hairy Major said, " that they're giving out special food and clothing coupons at Repatriation Centres."

The train moved forward with a shattering jerk. Once more the house where I was born receded into the distance.

The Repatriation Centre was two Nissen huts in the middle of a wood somewhere in Sussex. It was staffed entirely by escaped prisoners of war, most of whom we already knew. In one hour dead they had us medically examined, documented and back at the station.

"You get two months leave. Personally I don't think that anyone will ever want to see you again," said the C.O. He had been in the same squad with me at Sandhurst. "The thing is," he said, slipping effortlessly back into the idiom, " you look so very, very idul."

CHAPTER TWO

AN AFTERNOON AT THROTTLE AND FUMBLE

"IT'S NOT the slightest use hanging about here all day doing nothing," my mother said firmly. "You're becoming demoralised." She had come into the bedroom where I was skulking unhappily for what she called "a little talk".

My leave was not proving to be as pleasant as I had expected it to be. Most of the girls I knew were in jobs they refused to discuss, alleging that they were "secret". (At that time it was fashionable to be in something secret even though you were issuing camp beds at the White City.) By day I had been forced back on the company of a succession of predatory widows, who drew false hope from my air of melancholy and who listened with awe to the rumbling noises made by a stomach which had been unable to stand the strain of liberation. My friends all seemed to be prisoners of war, busy like me nursing their private neuroses and we had so much in common that we used to cross the road to avoid meeting one another.

Even the Army seemed to have lost interest. Four days after I arrived home I received a letter from a remote camp in Ayrshire. It was signed by the Adjutant and ordered me to report there forthwith for posting. Someone who knew the place told me that it was in a bog ten miles from a railway station. I disregarded the letter. Every Friday for two months I received a letter from the Adjutant. It was always the same letter, except for the date and no reference was ever made to the previous ones. Finally they ceased altogether. I felt slighted.

"I'm very worried about you," said my mother, sitting

down on the edge of the bed. "I've been speaking to your father and we both think that you must do *something*."

"I am doing something."

She wasn't listening. "We're sending you to Sheffield," she said, "with the Gown Collection. Mr. Wilkins is ill." (Mr. Wilkins was the Traveller.) "There's a new Buyer at Throttle and Fumble. She hasn't been in to see us this season and we can't afford to lose the account."

Here I must explain that my parents were in the wholesale business, what is known in the trade as "The Better End". Twice a year, Summer and Winter, they made a collection of Models, based until the war came, on something that was supposed to have happened in Paris (what heavier industries call prototypes), and invited the buyers of the big department stores and smaller enterprises, called "Madam Shops", to visit London and place an order for the coming season. But not all the buyers came to London and some of those who did would pass my parents by. It then became necessary to stalk them on their own ground and make a killing there—this was where Mr. Wilkins came in, but Mr. Wilkins was ill.

I was not in the business myself and knew nothing about it but now my mother had me cornered. I couldn't think of any reason why I shouldn't go.

"You can take Bertha," she added, "to show the gowns."

Bertha was a free-lance model my parents employed to display their outsize clothes so that the buyers could make their choice under battle conditions. I had first met Bertha some weeks previously at a fashion show at a London hotel at which our firm was "showing". My mother had insisted on me attending it on the grounds that "it would cheer me up". Bertha was very outsize indeed and grunted as she eased herself down at our table after the show. She had fat little feet of which she was inordinately proud and quite soon Bertha was massaging my ankles with them under the table, like a mare scratching itself against an old post. I was absorbed in studying the model girls employed by less-specialised firms, who looked like racehorses, and in wishing that we were showing small sizes. Before she left, unasked she wrote her telephone number on my programme.

"I'll do anything," I said, "as long as it's not with Bertha."

"Then you'll have to show them on the hangers," said my mother. She sounded vexed. "But they won't look the same without Bertha. She's such a willing girl."

"I know, that's why I'd rather show them in the hand."

"I think it will do you good to get away, dear," my mother said, as she got up to go, triumphant as usual. "Oh, and by the way, a Mrs. Bassett has telephoned three times already. I said you were asleep."

Two days later I arrived in Sheffield, by train. I was wearing a pre-war suit that was so full of moth holes when I first put it on that it looked as though it had been peppered with shot. My mother had had it neatly repaired in the workroom with wool of an odd shade of blue.

It was raining steadily and although it was only eleven o'clock in the morning the sky was almost as dark as night. With me were four enormous wicker baskets, things called "skips", which contained the Gown Collection.

"Commercial?" demanded the man at Left Luggage. He was a gloomy-looking, hollow-eyed fellow. If it was always like this it was difficult to see how he could have looked otherwise.

"No," I said. At this stage I was sensitive about my amateur status. "Have it your own way," he said. "Cheaper if they're Commercial. It's all the same to me if they're full of corpses," and gave me a ticket.

My father had written to Throttle and Fumble announcing

that "Our Mr. Newby will be calling on you," but no reply had been received when I left London, so I telephoned.

"Throttle and Fumble," a voice said at the other end and I pressed Button A. There was a click and I was disconnected. All attempts to gain the attention of the operator failed.

There was an interval while I bought a magazine I didn't want in order to collect some change and a further wait in a queue for a telephone.

"Throttle and Fumble," said the voice again.

"I want to speak to the Gown Buyer."

"Speciality Model Gowns, Model Gowns, Dream Girl Room or Inexpensives?" the voice said, archly. Confronted with such a choice I wasn't sure.

"Well, if you're not sure, I can't connect you."

"Speciality Model Gowns," I said, guessing wildly.

There was a whirring noise and a new voice said, "Throttle and Fumble, Dream Girl Room, Good morning."

"I want Speciality Model Gowns."

"Just a moment, I'll have you transferred." There was a succession of tocking noises and yet another voice said, "Sorry to trouble you, dear, will you transfer this call to Specialitys."

"Hallo, Speciality Model Gowns? I want to speak to the Buyer."

"I'm Miss Flagstone, the Under Buyer. Miss Trumpet can't be disturbed. She's having a Fashion Parade. Whom do you represent?"

"Lane and Newby of London. My name is Newby." Put in this way it sounded ridiculous.

"Oh yes, we had a letter about you. You should have been here earlier. We don't see Travellers after eleven o'clock, and Miss Trumpet has done all her buying. I'll have to speak to her. She's just going to coffee. Are they nice dresses?"

"All the dresses are very nice," I said.

There was an interval of five minutes which seemed longer. People were banging on the door of the telephone box.

"Miss Trumpet doesn't want anything unless you have something *very* special she could use in her parade."

"They're all very nice."

"In that case Miss Trumpet says to come right away. Don't bring a lot. And she doesn't promise to buy."

There were no taxis outside the station.

"Don't you know there's a war on?" said the porter, who was trailing after me with a trolley piled high with my wicker baskets. "Like Gol-dust. You need a Barrow Man."

"Barrow Man?"

"Chap with a barrow to push your stuff up to Throttle and Fumble."

"How far is it?"

"Couple of mile."

At this moment, a man appeared, pushing a barrow. He was a shifty-looking little man with watery eyes.

"Throttle and Fumble. Cost you a couple of quid."

It seemed a lot of money.

"Carry 'em yourself," said the little man, "it's all the same to me."

The immense load was transferred to the barrow. I rewarded the porter, I thought handsomely.

"What's this?" he screamed. Other travellers waiting for the taxis that were now beginning to appear turned at the noise.

"Five shillings."

"Five —— shillings! What do you think I am a —— coolie?"

"I think you're a —— robber," I said with a sudden resurgence of spirit.

"I'll take a quid in advance," said the Barrow Man, who was listening to this exchange with interest.

I thought of hurrying on to Throttle and Fumble to announce my arrival, but terrible stories of lost collections, recounted by my parents, made me stay with the Barrow Man. At first I walked on the pavement a few paces behind him but this seemed rather snobbish so I descended into the gutter and marched a few yards ahead with my umbrella up. It was like a procession.

"Throttle and Fumble," said the Barrow Man after an interminable journey.

The store was housed in an Edwardian building shaped like a hunk of cheese. It was difficult to see how human beings could be accommodated in the thin end of it at all. We came to a slithering halt outside one of the principal entrances at which a commissionaire in an absurdly pretentious royal blue uniform stood guard.

"You can't stop here. Round the back for travellers," he said. Then he looked at me again and said, "Oh, blimey!"

"Frognall," I said, "what the devil are you doing here? And in that rig-out?"

Frognall had been one of our less-attractive acquisitions in the Middle East. He was a boastful, drunken fellow who enjoyed dropping dark hints to his girl friends about the nature of the operations on which we were employed. In Alexandria, far from war's alarum, unless watched closely he went about armed to the teeth with fighting knives and a ·45 Colt Automatic.

For security reasons our unit did not possess a badge; each man wore the badge of the regiment from which he had been seconded. Frognall invented one, a tasteful design of crossed tommy-guns over a submarine, wreathed with the names of places on the enemy coastline which had been visited by members of our organisation in the course of their work. He had it embroidered in the bazaar. Frognall had left us in 1942; the last I had heard of him was that he had deserted.

"More to the point, what're you doing?" Frognall said belligerently, there had been little love lost between us. "Come down a bit, haven't you?"

"I'm selling clothes, Frognall. But what are you doing with all those medals." He was wearing the ribbons of the Distinguished Conduct Medal, the Military Medal and Bar, and the Croix de Guerre with Palm.

"Gottem in ther Resistance."

"You had to work fast to do that."

"I'm Sarn-Major Bodkin now," said Frognall defiantly, "at Throttle and Fumble."

"Well, when I'm back in London I'll remember you to the Commanding Officer. He'll be glad to know that you've done so well."

"I shouldn't do that," said Frognall, "towards the end I wasn't on very good terms with the C.O."

"All right, Frognall, we'll see. But just at this moment there's a nice bit of work here, carrying these baskets up-stairs."

Speciality Model Gowns were on the third floor. The lift was too small to accommodate us. We puffed up the stairs with the first basket, butting the shoppers with it, through the restaurant where the customers were gorging themselves on bilious-looking cakes, through the Dream Girl Room and into the Department.

At first I thought that it was being demolished. The show-room was full of workmen sawing wood and hammering away at something that looked like a packing case for an obelisk. One wall was stacked with little gold chairs.

"STOP!" said a great voice.

It came from a woman more than six feet high with hair dyed bright orange. I had never seen anything like her in the whole of my life. She was like a Valkyrie. The remains of such women are occasionally discovered, together with their consorts, decked with amber beads, stretched out in the bottoms of Viking burial ships.

"STOP!" she said again, even louder. "Where do you think you're going with that basket. SERGEANT-MAJOR, PUT IT DOWN!"

We let it fall in terror.

"Good morning," I said, "Miss Flagstone?"

"I am not Miss Flagstone. I am Miss Trumpet, the Buyer. Who are you?"

"I'm Newby of Lane and Newby of Flagstone . . . I mean London."

"I know nothing of you. I never see travellers in the Department."

"Miss Flagstone . . ."

"She had no right to tell you to come here. Can't you see that we're having a Fashion Parade? The Compère's arriving at any moment."

"I thought you might like to see something on a hanger."

At this moment a sound like someone keening over the dead rose from a little cubicle and a downtrodden little woman in a scurfy black twin-set came racing on to the floor, wringing her hands.

"Miss Trumpet! Oh, Miss Trumpet! He can't come! He's broken something!"

"Who can't come? Pull yourself together, Flagstone."

"The Compère, Miss Trumpet. He slipped on a marble staircase leaving the B.B.C. He's in the Middlesex Hospital. They've just telephoned."

Miss Trumpet had not battled her way to the buyership of

Speciality Model Gowns for nothing. The qualities that had got her there now stood her in good stead.

"I will not have a Commère," she said firmly. "We must have a man."

"Young Mr. Fumble?"

"Young Mr. Fumble is not fit for anything after lunch, as you should know, Flagstone." Miss Trumpet's eyes were boring into me.

"You've got a fine, deep voice," she said. "If you'll do it I'll show some of your models."

At three o'clock the Parade began. Great changes had taken place since the morning. The platform was tastefully draped and banked with fern and chrysanthemum. In the background a three-piece orchestra from the tea lounge scraped away industriously. Three hundred chairs groaned as three hundred women leant back to enjoy something for nothing.

"And this," said Miss Trumpet, towering over the microphone, "is Mortimer Fell of the B.B.C., who has come specially from London to compère our show . . . Over to you, Mortimer," she ended, roguishly.

I picked up the script. "The theme is ' Back to Normal '," I said. All through what would normally have been the lunch hour I had rehearsed it. During this time Miss Trumpet had displayed the gentler side of her nature. I soon came to the conclusion that being cosseted by Miss Trumpet was an even more macabre experience than meeting her in the normal way of commerce with, as it were, the gloves off.

Almost at once the first model girl came prancing on. "Number One, FROU-FROU," I continued, looking down from my eminence on the platform on to the bald head of young Mr. Fumble, asleep in the front row. "A neat little number, isn't it? Suitable for COCKTAIL WEAR OR GOING ON SOMEWHERE AFTERWARDS. (What the devil did this mean?) Notice the detachable halter and CLEVER BEADING."

FROU-FROU was followed by a terrifying looking woman of ample proportions with blue hair. A vintage version of Bertha. "Number Two, Mrs. Whistle shows TWO CIGAR-ETTES IN THE DARK, a gown suitable for the woman who is a teeny bit larger." (I recognised one of our own productions here.) And so on to Number Seventy. Number Seventy was the Wedding Group. This had been carefully rehearsed. The string orchestra was to break into Mendelssohn and rose petals were to be scattered. It was to be the climax of the afternoon at Throttle and Fumble.

Number Sixty-Nine, SOIXANTE-NEUF, went loping off. "Number Seventy," I said, "GREAT DAY." The band plunged into the Wedding March; but the Wedding Group failed to appear.

I tried again. "Number Seventy, GREAT DAY." Nothing happened. The audience began to twitter. From behind the curtains came a gentle mooing sound. There was still one more line of script. I read it.

". . . And that brings us to the end. Throttle and Fumble hope you have enjoyed seeing these lovely things as much as they have enjoyed showing them."

And young Mr. Fumble still slept on.

"Miss Trumpet has gone home," said Miss Flagstone, much later, as we sat together drinking tea among the ruins. "She was most upset about the Wedding Group. She's not coming again this week."

I asked her what had happened to it.

"Never you mind," she said, darkly.

"Did Miss Trumpet say anything about keeping any of the dresses? "

"No."

"But they're all covered with lipstick and the velvet one's split up the back."

"Ah," said Miss Flagstone, "That Mrs. Whistle, I always said she was a slut."

Next day I sent a frantic telegram to the Adjutant in Ayrshire asking to be posted abroad.

CHAPTER THREE

LIFE WITH FATHER AND MOTHER

L ANE AND NEWBY LIMITED, the family business of which my father was the patriarchal head and my mother a director was a commercial venture of a sort that is now extinct. By the time I visited Throttle and Fumble on its behalf in that first damp Autumn after the war nothing quite like it existed in the western world. Perhaps on the peripheries, in the coastal towns of Asia Minor and the Levant, a blurred pastiche of it might still be found in those agencies with British names managed by Armenians wearing grey flannel suits and club ties. In England it was probably unique.

It was unique because it was one of the first establishments of its kind—and now it was the last. In the nineties, when my father had gone into partnership with Mr. Lane, their joint venture had been a novel one. At that time the idea of expensive women's clothes being ready-made was almost unheard of. That a store buyer could be persuaded to visit premises situated in the West End of London, far from the vast, wedge-shaped warehouses that hemmed in St. Paul's Cathedral seemed a remote possibility. Nevertheless they prospered.

In 1945 Lane and Newby, by then shorn of much of its prosperity, occupied a house with an elegant eighteenth-century façade in Great Marlborough Street. The Partners had moved there in the Twenties when Regent Street had been demolished to make way for the buildings that make it such a dreary, open ditch and which are now being dwarfed by even

more outrageous structures. When they bought the lease
Great Marlborough Street housed solicitors and firms that sold
sheet music. It had not yet become the epicentre of that
spectacular convulsion, the wholesale fashion industry, a
dwarf counterpart of Seventh Avenue.

Mr. Lane, the senior partner, was no more. The dissolution
of the partnership and his departure from the firm had been
preceded by an orgy of litigation from which the Newby
faction had emerged in a state of near-financial collapse.

I remember seeing Mr. Lane on one occasion only; when, as
a small boy, I had been on my way to Wimpole Street to have
a gumboil lanced. With his great beard he had looked to me
like Moses.

There the resemblance ended. For Mr. Lane was a man of
uncertain tastes. His exploits were always referred to in
hushed whispers. In my presence words descriptive of practices
of which, at the age of seven, I had not the slightest inkling,
were spelled out laboriously by my parents in order to render
them doubly unintelligible.

As the years passed my father and Mr. Lane became very
distant indeed. Both were sportsmen—but of a different kind.
My father took his exercise in the open air.

My father was obsessed by rowing. When he was forty-five
he married one of his model girls, who was twenty-five years
his junior, not an unusual thing to do in the business in which
he was engaged; but instead of allowing her to gain the upper
hand and run to fat, as is customary, he taught her to row and
reconstructed her into one of the most stylish oarswomen on
the River Thames.

The best man, who was subsequently to become my Godfather, viewed the impending marriage with misgiving. He
was himself a dedicated rowing machine who had won the
Diamond Sculls at Henley and the Olympics at Stockholm.

He and my father were owners of a double-sculling racing shell which, when they were properly bedded into it, was one of the fastest things on the river between Putney and Mortlake.

It was not the union itself the best man objected to. He himself had married the previous year, probably because he felt that a rowing man, like an ocean-going submarine, needed the equivalent of a depot ship to return to. It was the implied threat to their partnership in the double-sculler that worried him. His fears were groundless.

The wedding reception was held at Pagani's, a now long-defunct restaurant whose knives and forks survived until recently in a public house in Great Portland Street, W.1, still the great throbbing heart of the dress trade. Only a few guests were invited. My father lacked the necessary courage to inform Mr. Lane that he was depriving the business of its best model girl; and in retrospect the wedding day can be regarded as the beginning of what modern historians refer to as A Time of Troubles. As nothing else could, the ceremony underlined the disparity of interest that separated Mr. Lane from my father.

As soon as the cake was cut, my Godfather suggested a work-out in the double-sculler.

"The train isn't for hours yet," he remarked. The honeymoon was to be spent at the Lotti in Paris, where the senior partner thought my father was going in order to buy models from the Autumn collections.

"There's plenty of time to get down to Hammersmith. It's just coming on to high water."

"We can take a cab," he added, improvising recklessly to suit the occasion. And they did. "We had a jolly good blow," was how my father described it when he returned to his bachelor chambers at Queen's Club, long after the departure of the boat train, to find his bride in tears, supported by her best friend, who had herself made the mistake of marrying the best man and could offer little but cold comfort.

In the following ten years my mother devoted herself to raising me; enjoying herself with my father after office hours and getting on with her rowing. She had abundant opportunity to get on with her rowing.

In the evenings on week days in the Summer, when he was not travelling with the Autumn collection, my father used to row in eights; on Sunday mornings he used to scull ten miles. This Sunday morning ritual was a great trial to everyone as he used to return to the house, which he had taken at Hammersmith so as to be near the river, at half past two in the afternoon, roaring for hot roast beef and Yorkshire pudding. Because of the timing we rarely had servants; even in the Twenties only the most feudal-minded domestics would wait until mid-afternoon to serve lunch.

This unseasonable food despatched, he used to order his motor, a modest open Citroen (he had a great dislike for ostentation) to be brought round to the door where the chauffeur loaded it with baskets containing "the tea". Then, together with my mother, who by this time was in a state of nervous prostration, we would set off for Richmond.

Even this short journey of five miles or so was memorable. My father was a back-seat driver in excelsis; at the slightest real or imaginary provocation he used to stand up in the open machine and deliver broadsides of vituperation at any other road user who endeavoured either to pass him or, if a pedestrian, simply to cross the road.

He himself had driven only on one memorable occasion. On that afternoon, returning from what he always referred to in retrospect as "my trial spin" he had placed his foot inadvertently on the accelerator instead of the brake when about to enter the garage and had destroyed the façade.

In the Twenties Richmond still preserved some of the idyllic atmosphere of an earlier, more leisured age, and on a warm summer afternoon the Thames flowing quietly at the foot of the hill had something of the quality of a painting by Claude Lorraine, an illusion that was heightened by the misty blueness of the shadows among the trees and the grotto-like entrances to the boathouses of the mansions whose gardens ran down to the river, which were overgrown with vegetation, dim, mysterious and cool.

My father's private boat was exactly what you would have expected him to own if he hadn't been in the wholesale business. It was a really big double-sculling skiff built of mahogany and beautifully maintained. In 1926, when I first remember it, it was already fifty years old and I was still using it in 1959 when an unusually oafish, so-called waterman broke its back putting it in the water; by which time it was over eighty years old. Now for the first time in memory our family is without a river boat.

It had fixed rowlocks and fixed seats, each with a perforated felt pad for the scullers to sit on. The sculls were the original set made when the boat was built and were the most perfect I have ever handled. The craft was equipped with a boathook, what is called in river parlance a hitcher—actually a paddle-cum-hitcher with a long handle, which was very useful for getting in and out of locks—and a mast and a sail which was never used. The only times we used the mast were on the rare occasions when we towed the boat, which my father and I sometimes did, employing a sort of double harness of webbing. But even in the Twenties the towing path along the bank of the river had ceased to be used for its proper function; horses were no longer employed to tow barges, vegetation had sprung up and our efforts at towing usually ended in our becoming caught up in a blackberry bush. Why we should want to tow the boat at all was never clear to me. My father said it made a change and my mother, who used to steer, took the blame when anything went wrong.

The internal appointments were sumptuous. Up in the bows there was a long, fitted cushion of dark-blue plush with buttons on it, on which one could lounge at full length. The seat on which my mother sat while steering had a plaited cane back like the body of an Hispano-Suiza motor car; aft there was another long cushion. The carpets were of fine quality and matched the cushions. The boat was varnished and was the colour of fine old furniture. It was lined out with real gold leaf and beneath the rowlocks inboard there were black and gold transfers of sphinxes' heads. On the bow were my father's initials. Everything had its place; the picnic baskets were specially made to fit the boat and there were mahogany table tops that fitted across the gunwales, with holes in them for plates and glasses so that the contents would not spill "in a heavy sea". If any china got broken replacements had to be specially made—a process that took months, even years, as the holes were of an unusual size. There were hidden lockers and drawers for such things as loose change and tickets for going through locks; there was even a wicker holster affair, similar to the things mounted policemen keep their truncheons in, intended to hold a parasol—my mother kept an umbrella in it. Altogether the skiff could hold five people comfortably for an afternoon. It was also a camping boat. Iron hoops fitted into brass sockets in the thwarts to form a skeleton frame over which fitted a green tarpaulin cover. By day this cover was brailed up, but at night or during bad weather it could be let down to form a tent over the whole boat. This produced a sort of half-light which turned the occupants a curious shade of green. The same kind of cover is still fitted to punts on the Thames. In spite of their colour, or perhaps because of it, punt covers have the property of making young Englishmen amorous which, under normal circumstances they seldom are, except in liquor at three o'clock in the morning.

Our clothes matched our craft. My father wore white flannel trousers with a narrow black stripe, turned up to show his black-and-pink club socks. He wore white buckskin shoes and he had a magnificent blazer of cream flannel with five buttons up the front. None of the clothes made by his tailor ever wore out. They belonged to a period before the First World War when a button once put on was on for ever. My mother always contrived to be extremely elegantly turned out and at the same time workman-like as she needed to be.

Normally the least sensitive of men to what others wore, my father was extremely put out if anyone turned up for an afternoon on the water in what he described as " the wrong sort of clobber ". There was an occasion when a detective from Scotland Yard was invited to accompany us. My father had an extraordinarily wide acquaintance and I think he hoped that the presence of a real live detective would please me. For days before I was consumed with excitement, but when he finally appeared, in scorching weather, the detective wore a black suit, black boots and, when he took off his jacket and waistcoat, displayed a thick flannel shirt and rather grubby braces. He lent an air of gloom to an otherwise happy outing. From that time onwards my father always referred to him in the past tense as " that fellow who wore braces ".

At Messum's boathouse, when we finally arrived at Richmond, there was always a tremendous palaver about putting the skiff in the water. An experienced boatman would be in charge of the operation and apprentices were routed out of the dark recesses of the building to help with the launching. The wicker baskets were stowed away; there was a great business of putting on and taking off sweaters; at the last moment the leathers of the sculls would have to be greased. Finally we were away, my mother steering, I in the bows trailing my hand in the water and being told to "sit her up" by my father, who was sculling strongly, "to get her up a bit" as he put it. He was shoving her through the green water—for at that time Thames water was not the barely diluted sewage it is today—past Glover's Island, that beautiful little island with the noble trees growing on it that makes the view from Richmond Hill; Eel Pie Island; Pope's Villa at Twickenham, and Strawberry Hill where Horace Walpole lived; until somewhere by the sluices at Teddington Lock, where the Thames ceases to be tidal, we would have our picnic tea.

In those days our skiff was not an anachronism. There were friends of my father whose private boathouses held at least a dinghy, and sometimes a punt and skiff as well, friends whom he used to salute and before whom I made my best efforts with the one scull I was allowed to use as a mighty oar. The only interlopers were what my father used to call "trippers", who came down on the bus from London and hired a boat for an hour or so. They were usually to be found in midstream and, if they were in a punt, happily paddling from both ends in opposite directions, trying to tear the thing apart.

It was not so much the social implications of their performance that upset my father, although the idea of a punt being propelled by anything other than a pole must have been repugnant to him, it was the menace to his property.

"AHEAD SCULLER!" he used to roar at some otherwise innocuous artisan who was intent on ramming him. "SILLY KITE!" he would shout, shoving the interloper off with his hitcher. To which the answer was invariably, "Sorry Guv!"

But as the years passed, taxation and death duties played havoc with my father's friends. Their incomes were much reduced and they shut down their riverside houses. And worse than all this was the development of The Engine. It became possible to *hire* motor boats. The occupants of hired motor boats were not people who knew their place as far as the river was concerned, but aggressive young men anxious to show off in front of their girls. Cries of "AHEAD MOTOR BOAT!" meant nothing to them. Once one of them rammed us. There were no cries of "Sorry Guv", only a loud blowing of raspberries and the need to re-varnish the boat. On one occasion my father impaled one of these opponents with his hitcher-cum-paddle and only his rage and undoubted physical strength saved us all from a ducking. But it was not until someone laughed at him and shouted "By Gad, Sir!" in parody of some retired Colonel, that he decided to seek shelter higher up the river.

Once a year we used to have a week's camping on the river between Windsor and Henley. It was a complicated and awesome operation. For weeks beforehand equipment considered necessary to our comfort was assembled in a spare room: travelling rugs smelling of moth balls, hurricane lanterns, shovels for digging holes in fields and, at the last moment, veal and ham pies with designs of thistles and acorns worked in the crust, cold Scotch ribs of beef, tins of fruit salad, bottles of hock, glasses of tongue.

We used to arrange to be towed upstream as far as Staines. It was always a mystery to me that my father, who had such an abiding sense of propriety so far as the river was concerned, could risk his vessel in such a hair-brained way, but he did; and no accident ever befell us.

On the day of the tow we used to hang about in mid-stream (just like the trippers) waiting for the steamer to come up from Richmond Bridge. As she surged past bells rang, hundreds of eyes gazed down on us and my father threw a specially prepared line to someone hanging over the stern. There was a tremendous jerk and we would be off, with the bow high out of the water, the skiff yawing horribly until my mother got the hang of the steering. The locks were a nightmare. It was my job to fend the steamer off and stop her from squashing us against the slimy, green walls.

All sorts of ludicrous adventures befell us on these holidays. My father was seldom good-tempered since he was either averting disasters or participating in them: like the time at a delightful, Arcadian place called Aston Ferry, when he discovered that we were moored near a wasp's nest and insisted on smearing the bottom of a frying pan with jam to "attract the beggars". We soon found ourselves rowing for our lives in mid-stream, having abandoned our equipment, as heavily engaged as a convoy in the Coral Sea. It was difficult to feel sorry for my father when he was stung on the nose.

Generally it rained. The rain in the Thames Valley is like the tropical downpour in some fever-ridden jungle, but more intense. And there were swans, made friendly by my mother, who used to give them sardine sandwiches. My father would mistake their intentions.

"Strong enough to pull you under, those beggars," he would observe, lunging at them with the hitcher; dismayed by this unfriendly reception they would raise themselves in the water and hiss ferociously.

In July, 1937, we were on our way downstream, bound for Richmond after Henley Regatta. We arrived very damp at Bray, a village once famous for its vicar, latterly for the Hind Head Hotel, which at that time had one of the finest cellars in England. We had an excellent dinner. My father drank burgundy and my mother drank claret (this was one of the provinces in which he never succeeded in subordinating her tastes to his own).

My father decided that he liked Bray. It was also a very wet night. We never went back to Richmond; the boat was hauled out and put in the boathouse. My father had had enough.

At Bray all went well for a bit; but in the long run affluent members of his own trade, in electric canoes, and the Guards Boat Club at Maidenhead proved too much for him. A knowledge of watermanship is not one of the conditions of membership of the Brigade of Guards. The members of the Boat Club who drifted across my father's course purveyed a brand of ill-manners that was unequalled in the civilised world and for which he was no match.

"You don't find many young fellows interested in skiff work down here," he remarked one evening as we were easing the boat in to the landing stage after a particularly disagreeable encounter. "I think I'll move her up next year." He meant to Henley, the last stronghold of the rowing man.

It was July 1939. Fifteen years were to elapse before he was able to put his plan into operation.

CHAPTER FOUR

OLD MR. NEWBY

IF I have dealt at what may seem unnecessary length with my father's addiction to rowing it is because, seeing his life in retrospect, I realise that it meant more to him than any other part of it.

My father was a complex man. With his love of active sport and the pleasure he derived from the good things of life there was coupled a deep, Victorian sense of guilt that he never succeeded in throwing off. It partly sprang from a deep-rooted conviction that no one should enjoy life as much as he did and partly from a feeling that he was not cultivating his garden with the same assiduity as some of his fellows; those now elderly men who before 1914 had fled from the pogroms of Eastern Europe and set themselves up as tailors in the East End of London.

Working sixteen hours a day, knowing only a minimal amount of English, the most forceful of these refugees had succeeded in setting their sons and daughters on the road to a way of life which to them, working in their sweat shops, must have seemed a crazy dream. In the Thirties their children and grandchildren were beginning to reap the harvest which they themselves had sown with toil and tears—the showroom in Margaret Street, the family house in Cricklewood, the weekends at Cliftonville and Hove, the grandchildren down for Westminster and St. Paul's. It was these men who had trodden the muddy streets of Lvov, Kovel and Voronezh often in fear and trembling who laid the foundations on which the British Rag Trade was raised.

My father was on excellent terms with these old men, many of whom he had employed as outside tailors at the time of the Siege of Sidney Street. A lesser man might have permitted himself a slight feeling of jealousy. If he did experience such feelings he never betrayed them. They too, in their own way, were extremely fond of him. Many of them had suffered fearful indignities and for this reason were at times slightly incredulous at his attitude (to someone who has been unsuccessfully sabred by a Cossack a display of tolerance is often equated with feeble-mindedness). Because he was so English and intolerant in many ways it was one of the last things that one might have expected of him. It was a contradiction in his character that he was only half-aware of, but one that gave him considerable pleasure. In a world that was becoming increasingly racially conscious, among the people with whom he did business his name was a by-word, a sort of laisser-passer.

He never, however, lost his inborn ferocity. There was an occasion when he picked up a man who was behaving in an objectionable fashion on his premises and threw him headlong into the street. The victim brought an action against my father for assault and battery. My father was put in the box and cross-examined by his opponent's lawyer—an extremely didactic individual.

"Tell the Court what you actually did to my client, Mr. Newby.'

"I ejected him from my premises," my father said.

"Oh, you ejected him did you? Perhaps you would be good enough to give an ocular demonstration of what you actually did to my client? "

"I did this," said my father. He leant forward and gave the lawyer a violent shove in the chest so that he sat down on the floor.

At this there was a great uproar. The lawyer, his client forgotten, rose to his feet himself claiming assault and battery.

"Well, Mr. Smallbones," said the Judge looking down from his eminence. "You can hardly complain. You asked for an ocular demonstration—and you got it. The whole thing is absurd. The case is dismissed."

My father was much disturbed by the political state of the country and by the decline in religious observance. He had a deep-rooted regard for the established order of a religion which he never publicly practiced. He never entered a church except as a tourist to look at some family vault.

Yet he would spend long periods on Sunday mornings before setting off for the rowing club reading interminable articles to my mother and me on the parlous state of the Church of England. *The Observer* was not the free-thinking organ that it is today. If it had been, in all probability he would have burned it ritually.

My mother bore these diatribes with fortitude. She had long since cultivated an expression of eager interest which she was able to assume for long periods of time whilst allowing her mind to range on more attractive subjects. He used to try and catch her out by stopping suddenly in the middle of a sentence, but she was equal to this.

"Why don't you go on, dear?" she would say, blandly, sipping her lapsang souchong. My father would look daggers at her and perforce continue.

I was not so clever. As I grew older it became more difficult for me to listen with equanimity to a twenty-minute reading of a leading article by J. L. Garvin on *The Decline of Imperial Responsibility* with intervals in which my father made plain his own point of view, and as a result our relationship deteriorated.

He had a curious obsession with violence, but it was of an abstract kind. Walking along a beach he would come on a piece of wood made smooth by long immersion in the water. "Foo!" he would say, weighing it in his hand. "You could give a wrong 'un a good slosh with that."

And his house was full of weapons of offence. Life preservers made from cane and lead and pigskin from Swaine and Adeney, shillelaghs from the bogs and odd lengths of lead piping which he had picked up on building sites. "This might do," he would say and add it to his collection. But there was nothing eerie about this obsession. He was not addicted to canings and flagellation. "Silly kite," was all he used to say to me when roused, "You deserve a thick ear!" and at the same time delivered it.

So far as his business was concerned my father travelled a good deal—whenever possible in such a manner that he would arrive back in time for his Sunday morning row—after the departure of Mr. Lane he usually had my mother in tow. She accompanied him "to put the things on". She also did most of the packing and unpacking. When he went to Paris or Berlin to buy models for copying she helped him to make up his mind. Sometimes they used to set off for a mysterious place called the Hook in order to sell gigantic coats to the Dutch.

They were both assiduous letter writers and to this day I possess what must be an almost unique collection of letter headings from the Grand Hotels of Europe, stretching from Manchester to Budapest. "We had a most disagreeable journey, dear," my mother wrote, "from Liverpool Street to Harwich, where you would have enjoyed seeing the destroyers. The ship was very dirty and draughty and everybody was sick except your father." With the letter arrived a box of sweets from Amsterdam that tasted of coffee beans.

They rarely travelled by air. My father had been a pioneer air traveller on Imperial Airways until on one occasion the machine in which he had been travelling had got into an air pocket and fallen vertically a hundred feet before regaining its equilibrium. The shock had been so great that my father's head had gone clean through the roof and he had found himself in a screaming wind looking straight into the monocled eye of Sir Sefton Brancker, the Director of Civil Aviation, who had suffered a similar indignity. After the forced landing in a field near Romney Marsh, Sir Sefton had stood my father a bottle of champagne, but he had had enough of aeroplanes and his subsequent journeys were made by more conventional means.

My father's letters were full of information, but declamatory. More like a Times Leader. "Be true to yourself," he wrote when I was in the Lower Fifth at the age of eight. "I hope you are getting on well with your boxing. When we last had a spar together I did not think that you were leading properly with your right." This was not at all surprising as I was left-handed and my father had made me change from left to right-handed writing on the grounds that left-handed men, "Cack-handers" as he called them, were not acceptable in the world of commerce. Because of this for three months I wrote inside out and the results could only be deciphered with the aid of a mirror.

A minor obsession was his preoccupation with my respiratory system. "You should sniff up a little salt and water each morning in order to clear your passages," was an injunction that was never absent from his correspondence with me. For more than thirty years I religiously avoided practising this disagreeable operation but after his death some inward voice impelled me to follow his advice. As a result I contracted sinusitis and I was told by the specialist whom I consulted that this was an outmoded exercise that led to acute inflammation of the nasal cavities.

But however sombre the counsels contained in his letters he always ended them with a little joke or two to cheer me up. He was never at a loss for a little joke. He used to keep them, or rather the bones of them in neat columns on the backs of envelopes, of which he had an inexhaustible supply, which bore the letter heading of the Hotel Lotti in Paris.

This collection was one of his few legacies to me. The envelopes give the beginning of the joke, some of the attendant circumstances but nothing that would make it possible to deduce the joke itself. "Three men in a Turkish Bath—One Fat—It's Pancake Day." Even now no one knows what was intended. To future generations they will prove as tantalising as the Rosetta Stone once was.

But not so tantalising as the visiting card which reads: Thos. W. Bowler (and an address at Walton-on-Thames) and on which my father had written in pencil in his neat handwriting "Met on train. Originator of the Bowler Hat?"

Another legacy was a set of dumb bells, weights and chest-expanders. At one time in the Nineties my father had been a pupil of Eugene Sandow, the strongest man in the world, who had opened a school of physical culture in the Tottenham Court Road. Sandow really was immensely strong. Eventually, at a time when motor cars were extremely heavy, he destroyed himself by lifting his own motor car out of a ditch into which he had accidentally driven it.

My father's capabilities at the beginning and end of the course were embalmed in a small, morocco bound volume. *Records of Development, Etc., Obtained During Three Months' Course at Sandow's Residential School of Physical Culture*. Although the units of measurement employed are not recorded, the numerical increases are so impressive that it seems certain that my father must have graduated with honours.

Harness Lift:	200	After Three Months:	800
Double-handed Bar-Bell			
Press:	80	After Three Months:	120
Arms:	20	After Three Months:	30
		(Can this be length?)	
Wrist Exerciser:	3	After Three Months:	8

What would he have emerged like if he had been a "resident pupil"?

All these instruments were made from a rustless, golden-coloured metal. The dumb bells were so heavy that when I inherited them after his death I found that I was unable to lift them in the manner prescribed by the instruction book. The compression and expansion of the springed instruments was also beyond me. This in spite of having myself been prepared for the business of being an "all-rounder". Long before the age when English boys are subjected to this kind of treatment I was made to have cold baths and taken for what my father described as a "jog-trot" along the towing path from Hammersmith to Putney and back early in the morning when no sane person was about. Sometimes for a change we would punt a football down deserted suburban streets, "passing" to one another. As a result I too acquired a strong constitution but the outcome was not what my father intended. I secretly resolved that I would not be good at games and I have managed to keep this promise ever since.

CHAPTER FIVE

BACK TO NORMAL

SINCE NO news had been received from the Adjutant about my future employment, within a week after my visit to Throttle and Fumble I was forced, with the utmost reluctance, to report for duty at Great Marlborough Street where, in the phrase that my parents were to employ with varying degrees of optimism in the succeeding months, I was to "learn the business".

"It's only a temporary measure," they said, "until you find your feet." They had a touching and totally unfounded belief that I was destined for better things. It was a temporary measure that was to last ten years.

As I pushed open the front door which was ornamented with a large knocker in the form of a ram's head, a little bell made a pinging noise. This I learned later warned the occupants of the Counting House, who also performed the functions of what would now be called "The Reception", that a visitor was on the way in. Before the war the staff had always used the side entrance, a nearly vertical flight of wooden steps which led to the cellars, when entering or leaving the building, but by 1946 such nuances of behaviour had ceased to be observed. As a result the Counting House was perpetually on the qui-vive—more often than not for no good reason at all. The cause of the bell ringing was most probably a junior from the workroom on the way out to expend one of her meagre supply of sweet coupons on a Mars Bar for the tea break.

I went in and as the door closed behind me the sounds of

traffic died away; the blasphemies of two vanmen who were unloading bolts of cloth from a pantechnicon and sliding them down a shiny plank into the bowels of the building faded; and I found myself in another, more tranquil world, almost in another century.

The hall in which I stood had white panelling; the floor ran first downhill, then uphill, creating the impression that one was intoxicated. To the left was a magnificently carved staircase which led by easy stages to the upper floors. The house had been built in the first half of the eighteenth century. It had been occupied by the actress Sarah Siddons and subsequently by that sinister personality Thomas Wainewright who was not only art critic, forger of bonds and wholesale poisoner but one of the foremost exponents of erotic drawing of his day, an art that he practised with such derivative skill that his work is usually attributed to his contemporary, Henry Fuseli, Keeper of the Royal Academy, whose technique was superior and whose imagination was even more perverse. On one of the upper floors there had continued to exist, until fire put paid to it in 1944, a small stage on which the famous actress had entertained her friends. With these two colossal personalities as previous tenants it was not surprising that the house had its own peculiar atmosphere.

My thoughts were brought back rudely to the present by the sounds of a telephone conversation that was taking place inside a minute booth under the staircase, so small that the unfortunate occupant had to choose between having a private conversation and asphyxiating in the process, or leaving the door ajar and delighting the staff of the Counting House as they pored over their ledgers.

Whoever was inside at this comparatively early hour had chosen the way of dishonour rather than death and was already engaged in an exchange of hideous confidences.

"No, Maureen! . . . No, dear!" said the disembodied voice. "No, I don't want to! . . . No . . . No . . . No, I don't mind *that*. I think he's ever such a nice colour . . . sort of bronze . . . I just don't like the way he . . . Well, he said that the last time . . . No! . . . No! The other one's worse than he is . . . I had to have it cleaned—— And my leg it was *all* bruised. Mum was ever so cross!"

As I listened fascinated to this recital a long, silky-looking leg slid sinuously round the door. Nylons were still in their infancy in Britain at that time or, in the jargon of the day, "in short supply". The owner of this leg had obviously overcome these difficulties. Attached to it was a foot wanton enough, as Balzac wrote, to damn an archangel, partially enclosed in a sandal with a four-inch heel. Half-mesmerised, as a snake charmer who has allowed one of his charges to gain control of the situation, I watched the leg in which muscles rippled as sleek and powerful as a boa-constrictor's. I could see nothing wrong with it. Either this was not the one that was "all bruised" or else the scars of battle had already healed. I began to experience that morbid sensation known to psychoanalysts as The Death Wish. For the moment I could think of nothing more delectable than being crushed to pulp by this and its attendant member.

Now the instep began to arch itself with infinite slowness, just like the head of a cobra when it is about to strike . . . Tearing myself away from this disturbing sight I went down the hall.

Suddenly a door opened that was almost invisible in the panelling. "'ERE!" said a great voice that made me jump. "Is that Mr. Eric? Mr. Eric! Where you bin? Your Dad's been asking for you!"

The owner of the voice was Miss Gatling, Head of the Counting House and Company Secretary. In the official hierarchy at Lane and Newby's she filled a similar position to that occupied by a Regimental Sergeant-Major. Ever since the time when I had been taken round from one department to another as a small boy and asked by various imposing ladies whether I liked school I had been terrified of Miss Gatling. And I still was terrified of her.

"Welcome to Lane and Newby's," she said, baring her teeth with a sudden accession of bonhomie that was most alarming. "There's a lot to learn. You've probably left it too late," she added, encouragingly. "I should get up them stairs and see your Dad . . . AND LOLA," she shouted down the hall, "WILL YOU GET OFF THAT TELEPHONE! YOU'VE BEEN ON IT TEN MINUTES."

"She'll come to a sticky end that girl. You'll see," she confided to me, gloomily. "Only thinks of men. You watch your step!"

My father's office was on the first floor. It was at the back of the house overlooking what had been the garden until Mr. Lane in an orgy of expansion had had it built over to provide more space for the business. It was a tall, narrow, rather gloomy chamber like a drawing by Phiz in A Christmas Carol. Originally it had probably been a dressing-room; leading off it was a powder closet to which one descended by a pair of steps. In the window seat there was a concealed wash basin made of lead, with brass taps that had been polished by so many generations of charwomen that they bore only a vestigial resemblance to taps at all.

In one corner was what my father described as "my portable desk". It was really a mahogany chest with brass-bound corners which could be opened out into a sloping desk. It was portable in the sense that it had probably been made originally to be carried on some African's noddle on safari. In it he kept old fixture cards which showed the breadth of his sporting interests before he took up rowing: Rugby football, cross-country running, boxing, swimming, wrestling and, of course, weight-lifting.

There were three pictures on the walls. One, a photograph of Lord Roberts of Kandahar, "Bobs" as my father called him, wearing a funny hat without a brim and looking angry on the rifle ranges at Bisley; the second a coloured reproduction of a rococo interior with a riot of cardinals at table "Drinking the Health of the Chef in Moët et Chandon"; and the third, framed instructions for "The Prevention of Fire in Private Residences", with an injunction under the heading GAS, "In the event of a leak send for the gas fitter and watch him carefully as he will sometimes seek for an escape with a light—and may find it at the risk of blowing up the building and all it contains!"

There was little room to move in my father's room, except to the window with its wash basin and to the roll-topped desk at which my father sat, for the whole floor was piled deep with newspapers. He kept every copy of the *Observer* and the *Morning Post* as they were published. In the cellars below they were piled high in the transepts, going back with their prophecies of doom and their sudden fits of optimism that were invariably wrong to a period infinitely remote, before 1914. What hedged him in here in his office were the editions of the last five years or so. "I remember reading something about it," he used to say when confronted with some topic that interested him and in the succeeding weeks he could be found, bent double, grunting as he untied the careful knot with which he had secured a bundle twenty years before, in search of the quotation in question. To my knowledge he never succeeded in finding what he was looking for, but at any rate he always found something else of interest that tended to deflect him from his original course.

Now he was sitting behind the large, shiny roll-top desk which he had occupied since the triumphant departure of Mr. Lane. As always, on top of his desk there was a large jug of barley water.

My father was now seventy-five years old. A serious operation of a sort from which few people ever recover had reduced him to a shadow of his former self. He had undergone it in an East End Hospital while the bombs were raining down, but he spoke remotely of the dangers to which he had been exposed. His former pugnacity had largely evaporated. Previously he had been a man of impressive physique; he was now extremely thin and fragile, like a piece of very old porcelain. But he was still exceptionally handsome and dressed as I saw him now, in a suit of thick flannel, with a rose in his buttonhole and his fresh complexion, he looked like a small boy who had been given leave from his preparatory school to attend the wedding of an elder brother.

"You'll have to get here a little earlier than this, you know!" he said, putting on his glasses and looking at me over the tops of them. "You have to set an example. I've arranged for you to start in the Coat Department—there's a lot of cutting off to be done. It's too much for Miss Webb; she's not as young as she was. None of us are. We need some new blood. Have some barley water."

"Everything's changing so rapidly nowadays," he went on, "I was having a yarn with old Brown in the silk trade." There followed a long anecdote about what old Brown had told him.

"But I mustn't keep you," he went on. "I've got to get down to Hammersmith—I'm having a new set of sculls made for my best boat. Shan't be able to use them much myself but you may find them useful. I haven't been at all well you know," he said, as if this was something of which I was ignorant.

"Well you'd better get on," he said, rolling down the top of his desk with a gesture of dismissal. "Oh, by the way; you know that shaving brush I sent you when you were in that camp in Czechoslovakia. Can I have it back?"

"I'm afraid it wasn't very strong, father. It fell to pieces."

"You young chaps!" he said, seriously. "You don't know how to look after things. That was a good brush."

It was one of my father's more maddening idiosyncracies that as soon as news of my capture had been conveyed to him he mentally wrote me off so far as the material necessities of life were concerned. In answer to my request that he send me a pair of corduroy trousers and a thick pullover he wrote back to remind me that such things were "in short supply" and that the civilian population of the island were having to "tighten their belts".

"I have been in touch with the Red Cross," was the sort of reply he used to send me in answer to such demands "and I understand that they have taken on the job of looking after your welfare! I visited St. James's Palace—the Headquarters —and there I was told that everything necessary is being done to ensure an equitable distribution of warm clothing and other comforts among you all."

It was useless to remind him that the clothes I wanted were already in my wardrobe and that there was no need to buy anything. He himself was the possessor of a vast and comprehensive wardrobe. Early privations had left him with an ever-present fear that he might one day find himself penniless and in rags. To counteract this possibility he became a hoarder on a grand scale. He bought leather bootlaces by the score for the heavy boots he got from Lobb. "I had these boots made," he told me once, "in case I ever have to take a job as a navvy,"

displaying a pair that would have been far more at home at
a shooting party in some ducal household. Whenever he was
in Paris for a week or so he used to order shirts, not as most
people are accustomed to order them, in threes and fours, but
in dozens. From these, and other forms of expensive haber-
dashery, ties, fine suits of underwear and silk socks, on his
return he used to select one or two examples for present use.
The rest were filed away in their original cardboard boxes in
which, embalmed in moth-balls, they would over a period of
twenty years or so undergo a gradual process of dissolution.

In this matter of sending me supplies my mother was in
despair. She used sometimes to send me a parcel clandestinely
but more often than not its existence was detected by my
father before she was able to send it off—as a result it never
left the country at all. Only in the case of the shaving brush
was my mother adamant. "The boy must be able to shave,"
she said.

My father grumbled a lot, but in the end rooted among his
possessions until he found a shaving brush of the rather primi-
tive sort that professional barbers use, with the handle dipped
in pitch and wrapped round with string. He added a suit of
silk and wool underwear for good measure that he had bought
in Paris in 1904.

I received this parcel in the wilds of Bohemia in the Spring
of 1943. The shaving brush was much admired by my companions but unfortunately it disintegrated the first time it was
put into water; the underwear even failed to survive the
routine check which the Germans carried out in order to
satisfy themselves that nothing illicit was being sent us. As
the Feldwebel held up the fully-fashioned silk and wool long
underpants with the Original label Edouard et Butler, Place
Vendôme, still on them they disintegrated before my eyes and
fell to nothing in a fine powder.

CHAPTER SIX

IN THE MANTLES

"IT'S QUITE easy really, Mr. Eric," said Miss Webb, the stock-keeper of the Coat Department when I reported to her after the interview with my father. "All you have to do is look at the docket. It gives you the number of the piece and the colour. You either have to get it down from there," she pointed to the shelves above our heads on which rolls of material, done up in brown paper, lay one on top of one another like giant chrysalids, "Or else it's on the floor." We were standing together in a sea of material and torn paper. "If it's not in the fixtures or on the floor then it may be in the cellar. If it's not in the cellar then it hasn't been delivered and it may not even be made."

I thought of the vanmen who had been making such a business of unloading a few pieces into the cellar when I arrived, and shuddered.

"All you have to do," she went on, "is to measure off the quantity that's written on the docket, and mark it off on the ticket, then cut it. You can either use a yardstick for measuring, or these." She showed me three inadequate-looking brass pins stuck in the dining-room table that was used for "cutting off". "I'll look after the trimmings, the buttons and the canvas and the linings, if you do the material."

The stockroom was very hot. It was mid-September and the Autumn orders were in full production. It was my job to cut off the lengths of material according to the dockets which had been written by the Department Manager and by Mr.

Wilkins, the Traveller, who was principally interested in the Coat Department. Together with the appropriate trimmings they would be collected by the tailors when they called on Fridays to deliver work that had been given out previously and also to collect their money.

I took up the first docket from a thick sheaf. It was for a single garment—a wool georgette, edge-to-edge coat which Mr. Wilkins had christened inappropriately "Desire". It was a special order from a store in Leeds for a customer called Mrs. Bangle. Completely untutored as I was it was obvious to me on reading the details of the order that Mrs. Bangle was something extra special.

"Hips 62". Bust 58". Waist 55". Neck to Waist Back 14". Upper Arm 19". Leave Good Turnings," Mr. Wilkins had written.

This seemed to make Mrs. Bangle a dwarf, $1\frac{1}{2}'$ thick. Even Mr. Wilkins had boggled at estimating the quantity of material necessary to construct a coat for such a phenomenon. "Wool Georgette GB. 14XX44/7. Blush Pink." These were the only details he had given. Funking the calculations, he had simply inserted a question mark and a couple of plus signs in the section marked quantity. The docket was intended for a tailor called Grunbaum and was marked "Urgent—Wedding—Seven Days".

I asked Miss Webb how much extra material I should allow. "She's a fantastic size," I said. "How did she get like that in wartime?"

"Bless you, Mr. Eric, that's nothing," said Miss Webb, "We have much worse than that. It's something to do with armaments. You'd better ring up Mr. Grunbaum and ask him how much he needs. It'll be good practice."

She gave me Mr. Grunbaum's number. I dialled it.

"'ULLO!" said an unhelpful voice.

"I want Mr. Grunbaum."

"Which Mr. Grunbaum?"

Miss Webb had vanished. I asked the voice to hold on and went in search of her. Eventually I ran her to earth in the cellar where I found her wrestling with a new consignment of cloth. She said I wanted Mr. Harry.

"I should have told you," she said. "There's Mr. Sidney, Mr. Joe, Mr. Harry and Mr. Lance—and Mrs. Grunbaum. Mr. Harry's the most helpful. Mr. Lance is still in the Army."

Lucky Mr. Lance I thought.

"Mr. Harry! Why didn't you say so in the first place?" said the voice, "'OLD ON!"

The sounds coming over the line from Grunbaum's were like something from the Dawn of the Industrial Revolution. There were whirring noises of machinery, a clattering of endless belts and sudden gusts of dance music that presumably were encouraging the workers to even greater efforts. After a considerable interval Mr. Harry came to the telephone. I read the docket to him.

"Listen," he said, not altogether ungraciously when I had finished. "What do you think I am? That Mrs. Whatsername; she don't need a tailor. What she needs is a operation. Listen, I'm telling you, I'm a busy man. Send her to one of those surgical shops. I can make six coats in the time I make that coat. I haven't got the labour. What do you think you can pay me to make a coat like that? You haven't got enough money. I'm telling you there isn't enough money in the whole of the West End to make it worth my while."

Happily he enlarged on this theme for some minutes. I was glad when Miss Webb emerged from the cellar. Without a word she took the receiver from me. Until this moment I had regarded Miss Webb, who was round and comfortable as a kindly, almost feudal figure.

"Hallo, Harry," she said. "Yes, very well, thank you." Without bothering to ask how he was. "Your man brought in twenty-two Floras this morning. You know what you've done. You've shone the linings. I'm sending the whole lot back."

Having put the ball, as it were, in Mr. Grunbaum's court, she simply stood there without listening while the instrument emitted a series of squawking noises.

"How much more material do you need for that special?" she said finally when he had exhausted himself.

"A yard and a quarter. That seems a hell of a lot. All right, send for it this afternoon."

Miss Webb thumped down the receiver triumphantly. "He can do what he likes with the others but this is Lane and Newby."

For me it was an exhausting day. Most of the rolls of cloth I needed were in the cellar together with the *Morning Posts*, the *Observers* and the last six dozen of my father's port, wines with resounding names such as Fonseca and Tuke Holdsworth, prudently locked away behind an iron grille. I made many journeys up and down narrow staircases, like a sherpa on the North Col. By the time five-thirty came I had run my shears through many dozens of pieces. Except when writing I was still left-handed. The shears were right-handed. The results of trying to use them upside down were deplorable; the cut edges resembled the temperature chart of a sufferer from undulant fever.

"I'm putting you on buttons tomorrow and you can do the carrying," said Miss Webb. "I don't know what Mr. Newby would say if he saw what you've done to all that stuff. He'd have a fit."

CHAPTER SEVEN

ALL BRUISED

THERE WERE three separate departments at Lane and Newby: The "Mantle" Department, the "Gown" Department and the "Costume" Department. (The firm's letter-heading still proclaimed to a slightly incredulous world that we were "Mantle Manufacturers and Wholesale Costumiers".) More than anything else they resembled tribal areas in which the aboriginal inhabitants lived cheek by jowl but insulated one from the other by their own magic circles. They were also prevented from impinging on one another by a fierce independence and by a fourth circle of more powerful magicians of which my father and mother were the necromancers and Miss Gatling and her Counting House staff the active familiars. Of the three, the Mantle Department, which was responsible for more than half the entire turnover, was the most potent.

In a world in which every square foot of space was becoming yearly more expensive, to maintain these vast areas was the despair of our accountants. Any reasonable organisation would have used one showroom for the short periods in each year when the clothes had to be "shown" and let off the others, but this was unthinkable in a firm such as ours.

These great rooms were surrounded by workrooms in which the original prototypes were constructed and by a labyrinth of small cubicles, vest-pocket stockrooms containing buttons and trimmings, in which single-minded enthusiasts pursued undisturbed, except at times of stock-taking, the same way of

69

life that they had always done since the coming of the internal combustion engine.

In my travels about the building in those early days I used to come upon them by chance. Occasionally a door would open for a moment, disclosing a grey-haired occupant happily engaged in counting sequins or hooks-and-eyes. Then the door would begin to close as an arrangement of pulleys and counter-balance weights filled with lead shot started to operate and all would be quiet as the grave except perhaps for a single, discreet cough. At such moments it seemed to me that I would never get to know all the secret places of this extraordinary establishment, let alone their inhabitants. I felt like an heir to the Castle of Glamis who had not been told the secret of the Beast which dwells somewhere within its walls.

But for the moment it was enough that I was the most junior member of the Mantle Department.

This was the home of Mr. Wilkins.

Mr. Wilkins was elderly, as impassive as a mandarin, almost bald and a complete mystery. In 1914 he had gone to the Kaiser's war as a member of a Territorial regiment; the following year he had been severely wounded in the leg by a sniper's bullet. As a result he walked with a pronounced limp and most of the time suffered hell with great fortitude. He had the capacity of making anything that anyone said sound like a brilliant idea without believing it himself. He even managed to give the impression that he thought my arrival was an excellent thing for the business, whereas I knew that he couldn't think anything of the sort.

Mr. Wilkins had two desks: one in the showroom at which he sat at the receipt of custom when the buyers were on the move; and another behind the scenes in the stockroom itself to which he retreated to do his paper work, brood over his expenses and think where he would go next.

He was extremely methodical and it was at this stockroom
desk which discreetly faced a blank wall that he sat, covering
page after page in his neat, minute handwriting, warning the
customers who had not yet paid us a visit that he was about to
arrive on their doorsteps. The formula he employed was
invariable.

". . . I shall be visiting Edinburgh on Monday, June 28th
with the New Season's Collection of Coats, Costumes, Two-
Pieces and Gowns and hope to have the pleasure of welcoming
your goodself at the North British Hotel at some convenient
time . . ."

He then went on to suggest a time that was more likely to
be convenient to Mr. Wilkins than to the Buyer.

He had a surprisingly robust sense of humour. The wall
above his desk was decorated with coloured postcards of a sort
that borough councils in the more squeamish seaside resorts
are trying to extirpate. One showed an enormously fat lady
in the sea smacking the bald head of a gentleman that was
just showing above water level with the caption, "Oh, Sir, I
am sorry. I thought it was my husband's behind."

It was always assumed that these postcards were Mr.
Wilkins' property. He never referred to them, but sometimes
he used to look up at the wall and utter a distant rumbling
sound, "Huh, Huh, Huh," that might have been laughter.

Most of the customers liked Mr. Wilkins, but now that he
is dead no one will ever know what Mr. Wilkins thought of
the customers or anyone else—or what he thought of the postcards. He possessed a degree of inscrutability that is rare in
the West.

The head of the Department was Miss Stallybrass. She had
been with Lane and Newby since she had started there as a
junior salesgirl and in the interval had acquired a considerable
presence. She was still sufficiently youthful for the epithet

"girl" to be applied to her without seeming grotesque. She shared Mr. Wilkins' capacity for agreeing with any proposition. Unknown to anyone she used to put down large orders for cloth for delivery at some date far in the future, secrete them under her blotter and suddenly produce them to the consternation of Miss Gatling and my father whose budget had not taken such expenditure into account at all. She was jovial, florid, had a laugh that made the chandeliers tinkle, loved parties and was as sharp as anything. My father liked Miss Stallybrass personally but always referred to her as "a chancer". He regarded Mr. Wilkins as much more stolid. My mother loathed Mr. Wilkins and regarded Miss Stallybrass as "full of go". Providing that neither of the Directors was incapacitated and unable to attend to business this partisan attitude of my parents was the most effective way of dividing and ruling. Together Mr. Wilkins and Miss Stallybrass would have been a formidable coalition; divided they were just manageable.

But in these early days I was ignorant of such intricacies; sorting my buttons and matching my linings, well-hidden behind the scenes I soon found myself prey to more disturbing sensations.

On my second morning, conscious of the disasters I had perpetrated, I was set to work on buttons and linings. Like a miser contemplating his hoard, I plunged my arms into large boxes full of buttons that were copies of ten-drachma coins from Fifth-Century Syracuse, all executed in black and gold glass and most of them different. When not engaged in the soul-destroying work of matching sets of four I matched satin linings with materials, most of which seemed to be in a dreary shade of brown.

"That's Donkey," said Miss Webb, helpfully. After having shown what I was capable of when left to myself she was seldom far from my elbow. I was immeasurably cheered by her remark. To me all the browns with which I was contending had the uniform tint of farmyard manure.

At this moment Lola, the owner of the leg, flounced into the Stockroom fresh from yet another encounter with Miss Gatling. "Coo!" she said, "I'm going to let my hair down." This she did quite literally by pulling out the pins which kept it up at the back in a style that was currently called Pompadour.

"Glad that's over!" she went on, letting it fall over her face and shoulders in a black cascade. Then her mood changed.

"Boo! You wicked old thing," she said peering through it at Mr. Wilkins, like a hairy Ainu. "And they say they don't know what happened to Jack the Ripper." As always, Mr. Wilkins affected to take no notice.

To me she was more genial. "Well you'll be a nice change," she said, squeezing my hand encouragingly, disregarding Miss Webb's monitory glare. She then spent a happy half-hour experimenting with her hair, twisting it into plaits and piling it on top of her head, all the time humming to herself in a mindless way.

In her high-heeled shoes Lola was almost as tall as the guardsmen to whom Mr. Lane had been so partial but there was certainly no other resemblance. She was one of those girls who was so remarkably silly that their silliness has a sexual quality that adds to their desirability. It was fascinating to watch Lola in repose as, completely absorbed in what she was doing, she wove her hair into ever more hideous forms. With her mouth half-open in what must have been an habitual expression, with slightly protruding teeth and moist lower lip, she had the almost half-witted look that some prostitutes cultivate in order to stimulate their clients. Across her face, as if the wind was ruffling a shallow pond, there passed expressions of impatience, sadness and a look that I was later to identify as hunger. She reminded me of a borzoi in whom Dr. Pavlov had lost interest half-way through an experiment.

At eleven o'clock there was a sound like a traction engine mounting a steep hill and Mrs. Smithers, an enormous woman as short as Lola was long, with great brawny forearms, came grunting up the stairs from the cellar bearing a tray loaded with "elevenses"—tea and whatever else she had been able to obtain on the special ration that was allowed to businesses such as ours. The traction engine simile was banished by her actual appearance. Mrs. Smithers' husband had gone down at the battle of Coronel and she herself retained an air that had something naval about it. With her bulges encased in a whale-bone corset that was as solid as armour plate she resembled a great sea-going monitor.

"Morning all," she said. "Let me have the tray back when you've finished, there's a dear." This to Lola who had immediately "perked up" (as Miss Webb said) at the sight of food, as though Pavlov himself had rung a bell in the laboratory for mittagessen.

As Mrs. Smithers and her ancient aides mounted the stairs with more and more trays of strong, brown tea and grisly pastries, the sounds of activity, the whirring noises from the workrooms on the upper floors and the sounds of typewriters beating out the monthly statements in the Counting House died away and Lane and Newby's ground to a standstill.

Although Lola's real surname was Topper and she lived in Muswell Hill, Mr. Wilkins always referred to her as Lola Pagola. Even to me it seemed far more suitable than Topper. In addition he had created an entirely imaginary world for her, as lush as a feather bed which he only allowed to spring to life when we were sitting together round the table which had been cleared for the elevenses or the afternoon tea break.

At other times Mr. Wilkins ignored her. He was aided in this twice daily by Miss Webb, "Webbo" as he called her. She showed a remarkable aptitude for this creative work which belied her homely appearance.

At such times the atmosphere was heavily charged with innuendo that it became almost insupportable. But Mr. Wilkins was so skilful in handling his inflammatory material that he always contrived to stop it from blowing up until the expiry of the twenty minutes which were allowed to us. The culmination was invariable. Mr. Wilkins having brought his fantasy to an outrageous conclusion used to perform what he called "the nose trick" with his tea; Miss Webb, by far the most mysterious occupant of the Stockroom would smile blandly; Lola would go into hysterics with her mouth full of cake and blow crumbs across the table with the despairing cry "Oh, Mr. Wilkins, you are awful!"; and Miss Stallybrass's voice would be raised in protest from the outer showroom where she took tea in solitary splendour. "Mr. Wilkins, will you tell that bloody girl to put a sock in it!"

Lane and Newby employed two sorts of model girl to show their productions. Professional, free-lance girls who were hired for a fortnight or so each season and of whom, thank God Bertha was an exceptional example, and those, of whom Lola was one, who either lacked the energy to make it a full-time occupation or else were the wrong shape. Besides showing the clothes when buyers appeared, these "permanents" put on finished coats and suits and "passed them" before they were sent out to the shops. Sometimes they found themselves being stuck full of pins when new prototypes were brought down from the workroom; for the remainder of the time they acted as showroom assistants with more or less enthusiasm.

There was nothing forthcoming about the professionals. The majority were so completely introvert that it was impossible to have coherent speech with them at all. There were two, Rosie and Julie, who were so narcissistic that they used to sit for hours on end as they waited for some customer to arrive, gazing at themselves in the same mirror, scarcely exchanging a word. Once a day they used to measure one another's behinds.

"You're a bit larger this morning, sweetie," Rosie would say spitefully, and they would both renounce their morning tea.

Some of the more juvenile model girls who brought a whiff of artfully contrived innocence to the showing of a white ball dress (Who the hell was having a ball in the Autumn of 1945?) possessed mothers of awe-inspiring appearance who used to wait outside the premises for their daughters in order to chaperone them back to Ilford. Sometimes they used to penetrate into the front hall where they sniffed the air suspiciously, fearing some contamination for their off-spring. One look at Miss Gatling usually satisfied them and they would drone on to her about the wickedness of the world and the unsullied reputation of little Annabel, who by the age of seventeen had a thorough appreciation of the commercial value of lascivious virginity.

Although she was employed to put the coats on and therefore had no need to undress at all, Lola spent an extraordinary amount of time stripped down to her underpants or else half inserted into one of her dresses—a writhing mass of arms and legs, like a female Laocoon. As a result she was always in a state of unreadiness for the simple chores with which Miss Stallybrass entrusted her.

"Lola!" Miss Stallybrass used to shout in her fruity voice and Lola used to pout and say "Bother!" and toss her head, the most wilful girl in the whole of Lane and Newby's.

Some minutes would elapse before Lola was ready to appear

in the showroom and when she did so she received a good scolding from Miss Stallybrass. So far as Miss Stallybrass was concerned it was only the shortage of labour, however un-skilled, that kept Lola at Lane and Newby's at all.

"You're in the wrong business," Mr. Wilkins used to observe with relish on these occasions to no one in particular, expressionless behind his spectacles. "You're wasting your energy putting them on at all. Huh, Huh, Huh!"

In those early days, whether by accident or design I was never wholly sure, I was treated to what were by no means fleeting glimpses of Lola's thighs over which were stretched suspenders in shades which varied between puce and viridian according to the colour scheme she was adopting; delectable buttocks which the bright, frilly underpants she wore did little to conceal—underpants bought at a shop at Shaftesbury Avenue on which were embroidered the words "my defences are down"; and perhaps most disturbing of all, her breasts, fantastic, unnatural protuberances that were in fact natural but which seemed to be constantly pointed in my direction. Her skin was of such a ghastly transparency that when I just saw her take a bite from a bun stuffed with synthetic cream I half-expected to see the fragments in shadowy outline, travel-ling down her gullet to the unseen regions below. But in the weeks to come Lola's digestive tract was one of the few parts of her anatomy that I was not given the opportunity to view at close quarters.

She even managed to impart a degree of significance to the eating of her revolting "elevenses". Taking a bite at a banana, at that time an article of diet "in short supply", she used to lean across the table towards me at a moment when the Stock-room was temporarily empty, wearing a tight white sweater that made me feel as if I was on the face of the Finsteraahorn and ask me in a voice in which even in my disturbed state I found it difficult to detect any passion, whether I wanted " a bit off the other end ".

I was more disturbed by Lola than I was at first prepared to admit, even to myself. The years I had spent in prison had been celibate ones; living on a diet of six hundred calories a day, except on the wonderful occasion when each of us had received two Red Cross Parcels at the same time, the lusts of the flesh were scarcely even a memory. Our dreams had been of great mounds of pudding; even the worst of us, rake-hells and near sexual maniacs, thought only of their mothers—and then only in the nicest possible way. Lola was nothing like the widows amongst whom I had been suddenly pitch-forked and for whose protracted ministrations I had been ill-prepared. Now, eating four good meals a day, like some Desert Father of the Fifth Century fallen from his pillar I found myself in torment and without the machinery of whips and hair shirts with which those early sufferers had attempted to rid themselves of a complaint that is almost always incurable, except by death.

My parents had led me to believe, when they had carefully steered the conversation into these channels, that the temptations to which I would be subjected at Lane and Newby's were similar to those experienced by doctors and could be resisted by something equivalent to the Hippocratic oath. " They're a nice, sensible lot of girls with no nonsense about them," my mother said firmly on the day before my induction into the Stockroom. After my first encounter with Lola I came to the conclusion that either my mother had a different conception of nonsense to mine or else she had deliberately obliterated the image of Lola from her mind.

It was slight comfort to know that my father was also conscious of Lola. Every morning and afternoon when he was on the premises he used to pass through the more lowly parts of his little kingdom in order to satisfy himself that all was well. On one occasion he discovered her wearing nothing but a red underslip and red shoes, like a demon queen in panto-mime who had just emerged from a trap-door in the floor-boards.

"That's a finely developed girl you have in your depart-ment," he said, looking at me quizzically, making me feel as if I had taken her on personally for immoral purposes—some-thing that I had been longing to do for some time—and went on to tell me how, when he was a young man, he had been left alone on a sofa with something of a similar kind in the front parlour of a house in Battersea.

"About four o'clock in the afternoon when we had the gas turned down the mother rushed in and began to tell me how happy she was that I was going to marry her daughter. I took one look at the mother—the husband hadn't even the courage to appear, he was squinting through the back of the door between the hinges—and I noticed that she had a small black moustache. I looked at Sophie, that was the daughter's name, and I saw that in a few years time she would have one too. I remember thinking it strange that I hadn't noticed it before. So I picked up my hat and cane—always a good thing to have them handy," he added, parenthetically, "and said 'Madam, I think you are misinformed' and left. But it was a close thing."

"I should take some exercise," he went on with seeming irrelevance. "A good long trot, then a rub down and a cold bath . . . Pity she's got such a miserable voice. Sounds like two pennorth of peas."

There was a moment of silence. "I remember the road well," he said, "It was called Sabine Road."

For the first time in my life I followed his advice and took up cross-country running. To my surprise I discovered that I had an aptitude for this lunatic sport, but as a moral purifier it was useless. As I toiled through the mud and slush in Epping Forest Lola's buttocks rose up before me through a haze of fatigue as just one more obstacle contrived by the organisers.

The wretched girl was everywhere; not only in the abundance of my imagination but in the flesh. She was even in the cellars, of course only by chance, when I went below to fetch up another supply of velour for Miss Webb, strategically situated in the narrowest part between the two main transepts, like a great sexual blockship. "I'll breathe in to let you pass," she said, emitting an insane giggle. "You'll have to breathe out," I said, idiotically. I was trembling like a leaf. "If you breathe in I'll never get by."

"I get so mixed up I don't know what I'm doing." Lola said, narrowing the gap. "Look, I've got an idea. You put your hand on my chest and I'll breathe in and out and then you'll know when you can get past won't you?"

"You know you're driving me crazy," I said some minutes later. I wasn't getting anywhere with the velour—or anything else. It was like handling a great warm blancmange. "Lola I must go to bed with you. Do you understand?"

"Ooh," said Lola, "Aren't you silly!"

CHAPTER EIGHT

SIR NO MORE

I T WAS not only Lola who was responsible for my physical discomfort. As a life-long sufferer from hay fever I soon discovered that I was violently allergic to wool. Hemmed in on every side by the stuff, which gave off clouds of toxic dust whenever it was disturbed, just like Mrs. Smithers with the elevenses I wheezed my way up the staircase from the cellars loaded with velour. Sometimes I used to slip out of the front door, the bell announcing my departure to Miss Gatling who used to come out into the hall and say " 'ERE ! Where you going? ", and gulp in the air of the city, but this seemed stale and tainted after the sinister fragrance of the forests of Middle Europe. The bones of London had been laid bare and the dust from the open bomb sites rose on the autumn wind. It swirled in the streets, old and acrid. Gasping on the threshold of the place where I was to find my feet I wondered whether I would live long enough to do so.

But I was uprooted from Lane and Newby's sooner than I expected. Ascending St. James's Street after a visit to my father's tailor who had been blown up by a bomb when passing through the Burlington Arcade and was if anything in a worse state of nerves than I was—the lapels of the suit he had made me had an edge on them like a fine saw—I saw a well-remembered figure baying for a taxi on the steps of White's Club.

I had been in the same prison camp as John de Bendern in Italy. He had been one of the first members of the Western

Desert Force to be taken prisoner when his tank had had one of its tracks blown off in an encounter with the enemy and had gone round in gradually decreasing circles until it had stopped completely. He had been an admirable prisoner, at least so far as the Allies were concerned. Not for a moment had he allowed his hosts to interfere with his way of life, which was at all times wildly idiosyncratic. With other members of the club in exile he played baccarat in one of the cellars. Stakes were high at the big table and letter cards intended for communicating with next-of-kin were used as cheques. They were invariably cashed in London on settlement day. It was said that one squire from the Welsh Marches had to sell his family estate in order to meet debts incurred in the cellar. A South African who thought the whole thing was a joke had issued a letter card that had bounced. The rumour ran that he was refused admission to his club when he returned home after the war.

"I've just come from Italy," said de Bendern, ceasing to emit the truly extraordinary noises with which he was trying to attract a taxi. "I've just seen Wanda. She wants to know when you're coming."

Wanda was a Slovene girl who had helped me to escape from the camp in which I was a prisoner, after the Italian Armistice in 1943. She had secreted me in the maternity wing of a small hospital in which I had been forced to take refuge with a broken ankle. During the weeks in which I had been hidden there she had visited me daily in order to give me lessons in Italian. This process involved a good deal of poring over textbooks with our heads close together and in spite of the oppressive chaperonage exercised by the nuns who were in charge of the place we had contrived to fall in love. When the Germans had finally discovered my whereabouts and had come to take me to Germany it was Wanda who had arranged my

escape in the middle of the night by the way of a drain pipe
and who met me half a mile away in a motor car. As a result
of her efforts on my behalf both she and her parents suffered
great privation and her father had been taken to the Gestapo
cellar in Parma which he had miraculously survived.

Our courtship, interrupted by my abrupt departure for
Germany and another period of imprisonment, also survived
and during the last weeks it had blossomed on paper notwith-
standing the barriers of language. My Italian lessons had been
cut short before I had done any written work and Wanda had
very little English.

"Come inside," said de Bendern. "There's a fellow there
I've never seen before. He's got some extraordinary outfit. He
needs people who know Italy. He'll fix you up."

Inside, just as in a play in which economy has to be
exercised in the number of characters, was Johnny X, the
young Captain I had last seen in the wood in Sussex who had
been with me at Sandhurst, now metamorphosed into a full
Colonel. The whole thing was settled at the bar.

"It's M.I.9," said the juvenile Colonel. "I can't tell you
any more about it here. You'll have to go to our place in the
country, to sign on." He gave me a chit for the War Office.

"Shuttle car's at four o'clock," said the elderly Major to
whom I was finally presented. He invested me with an aura
of secrecy which after some weeks of open-cast living in the
Coat Stockroom I found gratifying.

"Just sign this will you?" I signed a document which
threatened me with the most dreadful penalties if I breathed a
word to a living soul about what I was to see and do. As I had
no idea of what this was I was able to do so without com-
punction. "Plane tomorrow night from Blackbushe, I envy
you chaps," he said wistfully.

The shooting brake into which I was bundled through a

side door in the War Office had green paper pasted over the windows and the partition which divided the rear seats from the driver's compartment. I sat in the green twilight. It was like being in my father's skiff with the cover down. Behind me a moronic-looking soldier reclined on a pile of canvas sacks with lead seals on them. On the seat next to me was an even worse-looking specimen with Idle boots—Sergeant-Major Clegg would have made short work of him.

"Hope the driver hasn't got green paper on the windscreen as well," I said, trying to be affable. He looked at my civilian suit contemptuously. "Funny, har bloody har" I heard him say to his loathsome companion.

After an interminable journey the man with the dirty boots began banging on the partition.

"Go'er 'ave a leak."

"——! " said the driver. "Cancher wait, we're almost there."

With a jerk he drew up at the side of the road. Through the open door I could see a signpost that read Beaconsfield 1¾. We were on the A40 to Oxford.

A few minutes later we arrived at the great house* which was a repository of secrets of World War II. Secrets that had been acquired with great risk and sacrifice, then filed away and forgotten; secrets that by this time had worn pretty thin; secrets that had never been secrets at all. I was taken past a compound in which defeated German Generals, deprived even of the means of writing their memoirs for fear they might stab themselves, gazed at me disconsolately; along a path that wound through an orchard where the grass was waist-high, to a Nissen hut in an extremity of decay, on the door of which was a small plaque. The original inscription had been

* Now, I am happy to say, the Headquarters of the Army School of Education.

blotted out by a small piece of sticky label on which some orderly with shaky handwriting had inscribed the words M.I.9.

All the way from London I had speculated on the nature of my future employment. Was I going to fight out a duel to the death with the last of the S.S. in some eyrie north of the Brenner or would it be a search for the treasure that Mussolini was reputed to have left by the roadside on his last journey to the borders of Switzerland?

I pushed open the door. The hut was full of officers, officers with whom I had shared rooms in hideously inconvenient prisons in Italy, officers I had known in the Desert, the same officers who had greeted me at the Repatriation Centre in Sussex. I was given a hilarious welcome.

Johnny X came in. "Glad you could come, Eric," he said. "Nice to have chaps one knows, especially in this kind of show."

This was the moment. I braced myself. After all I really only wanted to see Wanda.

"What is this M.I.9?" I asked.

"It's been pretty secret up to now," said Johnny. "Actually all we're going to do is go around the areas we each know best in Italy helping people who helped prisoners when they were escaping. People like us. That's what you're going to do. That's what we're all going to do. For the first time for years we shan't be knocking things down."

I flew to Naples; begged a jeep from a friend, one of the great freemasonry of prisoners, and in bitter cold drove northwards to the valley of the Po. In the little village where I had been a prisoner, a village that nestled around an ancient castle, I found Wanda and asked her to marry me.

Six months later we returned to England. Together we had undergone every sort of indignity before we had finally been allowed to marry. Worst of all perhaps was the Wassermann test at which my fiancée took great umbrage, believing it to be a mortal insult levelled at her family. She came from the Karst, the wind-swept limestone country beyond Trieste where slights real or imagined are cherished forever.

"It is not the custom in my country," she mumbled in her fractured English.

I could hardly blame her.

"It's to protect you as much as to protect me, I have to have it, too," I said to her.

"I don't want to be protected from you," she answered in a hollow voice, exactly like an early Garbo film.

With the aid of John de Bendern who by now was at the Embassy in Paris she travelled to England in comfort. Unfortunately de Bendern having initiated the arrangements for her journey went on holiday to the South of France leaving the Ambassador in charge of their completion. As a result I received a testy telegram on the eve of her departure. "Wagon-lit *must* be paid for in Sterling. Duff Cooper." The Ambassador showed a remarkable prescience. It was many years before the unfortunate occupants of the British Isles were able to do anything else.

Alone she had to make her first contact with my mother. I travelled by a leave train that meandered over half Europe in its journey to the Channel, finally fetching up, as only a military train could, in a siding at Woking.

Demobbed at last I walked through the main gate clutching a brown paper parcel. It contained an electric-blue striped suit on which the stripes were only a little out of true and a curious green hat. Wearing it I resembled an elderly pederast. The shirt, the celluloid collar stud and the shoes that were as malleable as a diver's boots and some other items I had rejected.

On the advice of someone in the compartment I had given one of the Staff-Sergeants a pound note. "They keep a few decent suits hidden," he said. "Some of them are made in Savile Row. Even the good tailors have to make them." Now I was thinking of asking for my money back.

"OY!" a voice shouted as I turned right outside the gate. A very ancient private soldier was following me with as much speed as his ancient limbs could muster. "Wanted. You're wanted. Back in the Orderly Room."

The clerk handed me a large official envelope. "Sign here," he said. To him I was Sir no more.

I slit the envelope. It contained a letter from Johnny X in Italy. All it said was "Congratulations—Good old Eric, late as usual!" It was obvious that the letter had accompanied me to Woking on the train from Italy.

There was another envelope inside. It contained a single sheet of paper. At first from the letter-heading and the general lay-out I thought that it was concerned with some hitch in our Wassermann tests that had come to light too late.

"Sir," it read:
I am directed to inform you that His Majesty the King has been graciously pleased to approve the award to you of the following decoration: M.C.

You should write as follows, quoting your full personal particulars, including your personal number to War Office, C2 (Investitures) Whitehall, S.W.1., forwarding an address to which you desire the decoration forwarded.

I am Sir,
Your Obedient Servant
(There followed an indecipherable squiggle)
Director of Organisation

It began to rain. More in sorrow than in anger I picked up the packages containing my monstrous suit. The incident for which I was receiving this award had ended in failure. It would never appear in the history of any regiment unless cloaked in euphuism. Why, at this moment, nearly three years after it had happened, did I have to be given a decoration to remind me of the fact?

How different too was the manner of receiving it from my dreams of glory in the Chapel at Sandhurst on Sunday mornings when I used to sit at the foot of the marble pillars. In my dream I was to be decorated by Eddie the Adjutant, now a fighting General. (The King was unable to perform any further investitures. Even in 1940 it was said that his hand was becoming lifeless from incessant handshaking.) The Regiment—or was it a Division?—was drawn up in a hollow square. A difficult manoeuvre but we could do it. The trumpets sounded—not for the moment on the other side.

"I remember you," Eddie said. "A Company. Well done!"

There was another fanfare of trumpets. This time a rather dry peck on both cheeks from General de Gaulle, now miraculously restored to good temper, taking this opportunity to confer on me the Croix de Guerre.

Now the reality. The arrival of an official envelope with its bleak intimation that I was to write to C2 (Investitures) forwarding an address to which I desired the decoration forwarded. Dammit, they couldn't even be bothered to spell M.C. out! For this Sergeant-Major Clegg had screeched at us on the parade ground outside the Old Buildings. For this Eddie, the Adjutant had ordered a dog incarcerated in the guard room for being an idle dog. More in sorrow than in anger, for the second time I set off for the railway station and Lane and Newby Limited, Wholesale Costumiers and Mantle Manufacturers of 54, Great Marlborough Street, W.1.

CHAPTER NINE

GEORGE'S BOY

ON THE morning following my demobilisation at Woking
I left Wanda with my mother, who had taken the day
off for what she described as "a little talk", and for the
second time reported for duty at 54 Great Marlborough
Street.

Once more the doorbell pinged as it closed behind me
and once more, although I tip-toed past the door of the
Counting House, I encountered Miss Gatling.

"'ERE!" she said in her most audible voice after disposing
swiftly of the formalities of welcome. "You watch your step
this time. Just married!" She managed to make it sound as
though I had contracted some unmentionable disease. "They
say you fall twice as hard and twice as easily when you're just
married." A series of titters coming from the Counting House
showed that the audience was enjoying the joke, too.

I had had more than enough of the Mantle Stockroom and
of Lola. Wanda would make short work of her and I had no
desire to be one of the entrées in a Balkan carve-up. Long
before returning to England I had decided to ask my father
for a transfer.

I found him in rather low spirits but at the sight of me and
the problems I presented he soon cheered up. As usual he
dealt with these problems in an oblique way.

"I was delighted at the news of your decoration," he said.
"It's a splendid thing. By the way, what did you get it
for?"

"I don't know, I'm afraid. I think it's probably some kind of mistake."

"Do you really?" he said, eagerly. "That's what I thought myself when your mother told me. Bureaucracy gone mad. All those jacks-in-office scribbling away. Do you know, there's scarcely a decent hotel anywhere that hasn't got some kind of government department cluttering it up. If you're too busy I could write to the War Office and ask them what you *did* get it for. Then you'd know for certain."

"I don't think I should do that, Father."

"As you please," he said a little reluctantly.* "Everything's in such a mess at the moment. Look at India," he went on, moving effortlessly to his favourite subject. "We're giving them Self-Rule. Soon the beggars will be murdering one another in thousands. I heard at the Club that there's a rumour that they're thinking of giving Mountbatten India." (For my father and his contemporaries the world had come to an end in July 1945, with the victory of the Socialists at the polls.)

"Well, what about you? That's more to the point," said my father, abandoning the horrors of India as being incapable of solution in the time at our disposal. "To my mind you should be in the Showroom with Miss Stallybrass. The atmosphere's far more healthy than in the Stockroom. You'll meet the customers and if you keep your eyes open you'll learn a good deal. If you don't find you've got enough to do you can always call on some of the London accounts.

"Talk to Wilkins about it. You might even go to see X and Y." He mentioned the chairmen of two department stores

---

* Nevertheless he did write to the War Office. The citation, which he received after an interval, left no one in any doubt of the merits of the decoration, and re-inforced his own opinion of bureaucracy.

with whom he was on terms of easy familiarity. "They'll be glad to see you and give you some advice. It's worth while cultivating men like that. You can telephone their secretaries for an appointment."

My position in the firm was so ill-defined and the problems left over from my earlier service in the Stockroom were proving so difficult to resolve that I welcomed any mission, however unproductive it might seem, providing that it took me out of the building.

"Would it be a good idea if I got in touch with them right away?" I said.

"That's right," said my father. "Ring 'em up." He was so taken aback that I had adopted one of his suggestions without demur that he seemed to find nothing suspicious in my enthusiasm. "Oh, by the way," he said, as I rose to go. "Your wife seems a decent sort of girl. Pity about her religion. But it can't be helped. No good crying over spilled milk."

I thought it an unfortunate metaphor, and said so; but he seemed not to hear. "I bought this on the way in this morning. I thought you might like to read it. Wanda might enjoy it, too." He handed me a paper-back edition of H. G. Wells' *Crux Ansata*, a violent diatribe against the Roman Church.

"I'd like it back when you've finished with it," he said. And, with a hint of menace, "I've put my name on the fly-leaf."

I turned to the inscription. THIS BOOK BELONGS TO G. A. NEWBY. IT IS NOT YOUR PROPERTY! it read. Under it he had written his home and business addresses and both telephone numbers, rather like a small boy who writes "England, Europe, World, Universe" in a school exercise book.

Of the two chairmen, X and Y, X was leaving for America, which, for an inhabitant of the British Isles in 1946, was the equivalent of a journey to Tibet in 1900. Y, on the other hand, I was told could see me that very morning.

I was surprised by the ease with which I had been able to make the appointment. It was something that my previous experience in the commercial field had not led me to expect. Foolishly I attributed it to the fact that I was older, more a man-of-the-world. I was glad too that I was wearing my new suit, the one that had been made for me by the man who had been blown up in the Burlington Arcade, now re-constructed completely by a patient Italian artisan. "*Com'è ridotto il vostro Impero*," he had said wonderingly when he first un-packed it and looked with disbelief at the label in the inside pocket of the jacket that was adorned with the coats of arms of two royal houses.

At the vast store Sir Harold's name acted as a strong tonic on those members of the staff from whom I asked the where-abouts of his office. Vicariously I savoured the pleasures of power.

Even in the lift I was given special treatment. To the incon-venience of other shoppers, most of whom were women wear-ing hats adorned with regimental badges picked out in diamonds, who wished to stop at intermediate levels, I was whisked to the top floor in one: past China and Glass, Corsetry and Books, Baby Linen and Overdue Accounts, where firm but deferential men stood waiting at the receipt of custom on the thick beige carpet like pelicans on a mud-bank.

I arrived on time.

"Ah! Mr. Newby," said Sir Harold's secretary. In these few words she managed to convey the impression that I had done her an infinite kindness by coming at all. Her hair, which was cropped short like a man's, was dyed a fashionable shade of executive blue. She was the sort of secretary who, unprompted, sends flowers to her employer's wife and mistresses on a graduated scale of munificence.

I was ushered into the sanctum. The effect that it produced derived not from its contents but from its emptiness. There was a glass-topped desk, modishly asymmetrical like the flight deck of an aircraft carrier; a full-length portrait in oils of Sir Harold as Master of the Ropetwisters Company, and a very small photograph in a silver frame of Lady Y wearing an expression that I had once seen on the face of a bulldog that had been photographed for a recruiting poster for the Royal Navy, entitled "Dogged Does It". The only other item of furniture, except for a chair which placed the occupant at an immediate disadvantage by lowering his nose to the level of the desk, was an austere iron bedstead covered with an army blanket. On it the great man re-charged his batteries in an afternoon nap in emulation of a far greater one who had hallowed the practice by observing it. The air of the room was redolent of a thousand smoked cigars. That was all. There was not a paper, not a book in sight. It is with this panoply of nothingness that the great intimidate those wretches whose "in" and "out" trays are always bursting at the seams.

"George how good to see . . ." said Sir Harold, half rising from his seat. He and my father had been behind the same counter at a store in Oxford Street before going their separate ways. I was not what he was expecting at all. For a moment he showed his annoyance; then, with a supreme effort, he decided to make the best of it.

"You must be George's boy," he said, motioning me to the chair. "Your father spoke of you," there was a perceptible pause, "often."

"Well, you'll have to be good to be half as good as your father," he went on, as if I was not aware of this already.

"And what have *you* been doing with yourself?"

I told him in a few words.

"You'll have a job to make up for lost time," he said, as if I was personally responsible for this state of affairs. "You've left it late. We've got young men here, younger than you. Been through the mill here in the last five years. Been here since they were sixteen—know it all—not quite all, of course," he added, hastily, as if knowing it all in some way detracted from his own position. "Night school three times a week. Ripe for management. It'll take you five years to catch up. You'll be thirty. They'll always be that much ahead. Work hard, that's what you'll have to do. Jack-of-all-trades, Master-of-None. Doesn't necessarily apply to you of course," he added, conscious that he might have over-stepped the mark.

"There's nothing like starting at the bottom," said Sir Harold, pointing his great cigar at me. "And the world doesn't owe you a living. Two things to remember. George and I both slept under the counter when we were first apprenticed. He'll tell you. Only pity is he didn't get ahead like I did. Otherwise he might have been sitting here instead of me." He looked at me complacently.

I suppressed a desire that had been mounting in me to give Sir Harold what my father would have described as "a good slosh".

"I suppose you want a job?" he went on.

"I only came to introduce myself to you, Sir Harold, because my father suggested that I should. I'm learning the wholesale business."

"Ah," said Sir Harold, obviously relieved. "In the wholesale. Well, make your own way. Cardinal rule with me, never interfere with my Buyers. They know the market, or ought to. If they don't they get out—Sharp. Always remember, if your merchandise is right my Buyers will beat a path to your door. If not you go to the wall. Cardinal rule."

Naïve as I was, having heard something of the personal habits of Sir Harold's Buyers, I could scarcely repress a smile. Although they might beat a path to a manufacturer's door that path had to be sprinkled liberally with gold and champagne.

A buzzer buzzed, so softly that it was barely audible. Sir Harold bent forward over the framed photograph of his help-meet, patiently awaiting his pleasure in The Green Belt. For a moment I thought that he was going to kiss it in the manner of a sacred relic, but at the sight of its dumb devotion he frowned with distaste and addressed himself instead to an invisible microphone.

"Yes, send him in," he said. "Mr. Newby is just leaving." And to me. "Don't hesitate to come and see me at any time if I can be of assistance to you. I've enjoyed our talk immensely."

"What *have* you been up to, Mr. Eric?" said Miss Stally-brass when I returned disconsolate to Lane and Newby's. "Mrs. Locke-Smythson has been on the phone. She was absolutely livid. She says that apparently you practically burst into the Chairman's office and asked him why she hasn't been doing more business with us. She threatened to close the account. It's taken me half an hour to calm her down. I've got enough to do as it is with that bloody girl away."

I had nothing to say. There was nothing I could say. From behind the fixture which separated the Showroom from the Mantle Stockroom, where Mr. Wilkins had his abode, there came a sound that I already knew extremely well. Something that sounded like "Huh, Huh, Huh!"

As if this was not enough I received a letter marked "Strictly Private and Confidential", written in a spidery copperplate with ink that had been diluted with water. Its contents were highly alarming.

Dear Sir,

I have a matter of an extremely delicate nature to discuss with you. As the matter is one that, to coin a phrase, you would not wish to "come out", I suggest that we meet for a quiet talk at Lyons in Oxford Street at four o'clock this afternoon. I shall be identifiable by my bowler hat, which I shall be carrying.

                                        Yours faithfully,
                                        Ernest Topper.

There are eight Lyons teashops in Oxford Street. I hadn't realised this until I set out to meet Mr. Topper; neither had he. Once I found the right teashop the tryst was not difficult to keep. Mr. Topper was readily identifiable. He held his bowler hat in front of him almost at arms' length, as if it contained some noxious substance. He did not seem put out by the fact that I was more than half an hour late. He had the air of a man who was used to waiting.

Soon we were seated at a table at which there was only one other occupant. Mr. Topper now proceeded to reveal his identity. In doing so he quite unconsciously obtained over me a degree of superiority.

"As you know, I am Lola's father," he said, without preamble. So deftly had Mr. Wilkins woven his fantasy that I had forgotten that her maiden name was Topper.

"As I said in my letter I have come here to acquaint you with a matter of an extremely serious nature." His speech was a curious mixture of the jargon used by the doctors of forensic medicine to describe their gruesome finds, and the reports of court proceedings in the News of the World.

"I have reason to believe," said Mr. Topper, "that my daughter is in a certain condition. Furthermore, I am of the belief that a particular person, who is in a position of trust so far as my daughter is concerned, is responsible for having performed certain acts that put her in this condition. I have reason to believe that you, Mr. Newby, know who that person is. Who did it."

Not since the day at my prep school, when I had been beaten by the headmaster for a crime I had not committed, had I experienced such a sensation of awe and doom as I now felt. It was certainly true that I had wanted to " do it " with Lola, but unfortunately her own interest in doing it had proved more academic than real. The " certain acts " referred to by Mr. Topper were certainly not calculated to put anyone in an interesting condition except by schizogenesis.

" Mr. Topper," I said, with as much dignity as I could muster in a teashop. " I must confess that your daughter had a most stimulating effect on me when I first met her. Nevertheless I must tell you that I never had the opportunity to do anything that could have made her pregnant. You must have realised that your daughter is an exceedingly popular young woman. The Manager of our Counting House, Miss Gatling, will testify that she has an extraordinarily large following."

Whilst saying this I looked Mr. Topper straight in the eye. Doing so I began to feel sorry for him. He ceased to be a pompous ass or a potential blackmailer; suddenly he was just a worried father.

" You too," he said gloomily, alienating me for the second time, " I didn't know you were in it too."

" Will you kindly pass the sugar," said the third occupant of the table, an elderly person who had been so entranced by our conversation that he had allowed his tea to grow cold.

" I think we had better continue in the street," said Mr. Topper.

We stood in a light drizzle in Oxford Street, elbowed by

shoppers, most of whom seemed to be armed with ice-cream cornets.

"Mr. Topper," I said, "I object to the expression 'in it too'."

"I thought it was Mr. Wilkins. Your Traveller," said Mr. Topper. "He had the opportunity, didn't he? "

"Have you ever seen Mr. Wilkins? "

"I waited outside your premises at closing time the other night until he came out. He's the one whose got a gammy leg, isn't he? "

"What does your daughter say about all this? "

"She doesn't say anything. All she does is to complain about her stomach and she's sick every morning. It's been going on like this for a week now."

"Mr. Topper," I said, "I have only returned to this country in the course of the last twenty-four hours. Before doing so I was abroad for six and a half months. The symptoms you describe are those of the onset of pregnancy, not those one would expect to find in someone who will shortly be delivered of a child. I suggest that you obtain a competent medical opinion. And what about Mrs. Topper? What does she think? "

"She's been CARRYING ON," said Mr. Topper, "AS USUAL."

"Frankly," I said, "I think your accusation against Mr. Wilkins is absurd. Do you wish me to communicate it to him? " (Conversation with Mr. Topper was making me as pompous as he was.)

"Don't trouble yourself," said Mr. Topper. "I didn't really think it was him. I certainly never thought it was you. The trouble is," he said, nearer the mark than usual, "it might have been anybody. The telephone goes all day now she's at home—always men."

"Why don't you take the receiver off?"

"Can't," said Mr. Topper, "I'm an undertaker. We live over the shop."

The next morning I was called to the telephone to take a call from a Mr. Potter.

"This is Mr. Topper," said Mr. Potter. He sounded embarrassed. "I am telephoning, in the interests of security, from a public call box. You will be happy to know that we have had my daughter examined. There are no signs that she has been 'interfered with'. She is still 'virgo intacta'." He pronounced the words with relish.

I said that I was delighted. I asked him what had been wrong with her.

"Chocolate creams. Those ones with little violet flowers on top. Eating them in bed, right under our noses. Might have killed herself. We've decided to keep Lola at home for a bit," he went on. "The journey from Muswell Hill is too much for a young girl. She won't be coming back to Lane and Newby's any more." This with a sudden resurgence of spirit, by which he continued to make the firm sound a den of iniquity. "She's taking a local job, in the telephone exchange."

"Huh, Huh, Huh!" said Mr. Wilkins when the news was broken to him, officially. "That's just the job for her. Round pegs in round holes. Even she can't go wrong. Should suit her down to the ground. And better for us in the long run. Don't you think so, Mr. Eric?"

He gazed at me impassively through his spectacles.

CHAPTER TEN

A DAY IN THE SHOWROOM

"IT'S ALL very well your father telling you to stay in the showroom, Mr. Eric," said Miss Stallybrass. She was still suffering from the effects of the rocket she had received on my behalf from Mrs. Crosse-Smythson. "But it's difficult to know what to give you to do. You'd better sit over there." She indicated a small piece of furniture that was more like a prie-dieu than a desk. "At least you'll see what happens. Miss Axhead from Manchester is coming in at ten to put down her season's order. But I warn you she takes a long time to make up her mind."

On the first stroke of ten Miss Axhead arrived. She was a powerful-looking woman of about fifty dressed in what I was later to recognise as a buyer's cold-weather uniform; a Persian lamb jacket that was almost completely square; sheepskin boots worn over patent-leather shoes and an incredible hat with bits of Persian lamb on it, the left-overs from the sacrifice that had produced the coat, and a "little" black dress. Escorted by Miss Stallybrass she sank down on a sofa and, with a good deal of puffing and blowing, proceeded to take off her over-boots. I was introduced by Miss Stallybrass. I then hid myself as best I could behind my inadequate prie-dieu.

"That's a pretty brooch," Miss Stallybrass said, by way of opening gambit, admiring a hideous marcasite ornament in the form of a sealyham's head that Miss Axhead had pinned to her little black dress.

"That's my little Boy-Boy," said Miss Axhead, betraying

a depth of emotion that would have been difficult to deduce from her appearance.

An hour later Miss Axhead was still sitting on the settee. During this time she had discussed with Miss Stallybrass the Government and Sir Stafford Cripps; the sealyham which, by the sound of it, was ripe for destruction; the play to which she had been taken the previous evening by one of her suppliers, a rather gentle intellectual who, before the purges, had been a professor at Göttingen University, which she had not enjoyed; Christian Science; The Robe, which she was reading in bed and was thoroughly enjoying; several unpleasant ailments from which her friends were suffering; the discomfort of the hotel in which she always stayed when she came to London; and the iniquity of the Dress Buyer, her lifelong friend, who was cutting in on her territory by buying dresses with jackets and with whom she was no longer on speaking terms. Apart from the Dress Buyer there was no mention of business at all.

It was now eleven o'clock. Mrs. Smithers appeared for the second time with tea and biscuits. She had already produced a snifter for Miss Axhead when she arrived, which had kept her going until the main supplies were brought up. Mr. Wilkins emerged from his fox-hole to pay his respects to Miss Axhead. Adroitly, he asked a number of questions to which he already knew the answer, having been privy to the entire conversation. "Delighted to see you, Miss Axhead," he said, and withdrew with the air of a trusted counsellor.

My father arrived. He also discussed the political situation, going over the ground that had already been covered by Miss Stallybrass, but with more conviction, and told her one of his little jokes which made Miss Axhead laugh. He was followed by the head of the Costume Department, who had been hovering anxiously at the door under the impression that Miss

Axhead might escape her. Miss Axhead was also the suit buyer. During this time other coat buyers who arrived un- announced, without appointments, were siphoned off into Gowns and Costumes and Rosie and Julie made long and circuitous journeys backwards and forwards between the Coat Stockroom and Costumes, by-passing Mantles completely so that Miss Axhead should not be disturbed.

At twelve-thirty Miss Axhead was offered a gin and tonic, which she accepted gratefully, and at a quarter to one she went upstairs "to make herself comfortable" before going out to lunch with Miss Stallybrass.

Miss Stallybrass was dressed to the nines in a suit with a very pronounced stripe and a large fur cape. The effect was a little top-heavy and when she went to collect some petty cash from the Counting House to pay for the lunch, Miss Gatling asked her if she was "bombed out".

"I always enjoy coming to Lane & Newby," Miss Axhead said as they were leaving. "It has such a homely atmosphere. I feel I can really let my hair down."

At two-thirty they returned. I thought Miss Stallybrass looked a little tired, but she was still game and her laugh was as hearty as ever. Miss Axhead was full of beans and described her summer holiday at Torquay in some detail. At three o'clock Mrs. Smithers arrived with more tea and Dundee cake and at three-thirty Miss Axhead telephoned to another supplier, who had been waiting for her since two, to say that she was "held up".

She now began to talk about her "specials". These were customers who were either so rich that nothing sufficiently splendid could be found for them amongst Miss Axhead's stock of "models" or else were so misshapen that they needed something that was made-to-measure. All the details of these difficult customers were written down on several crumpled sheets of paper and from time to time Miss Axhead looked at them despairingly.

It was obvious that unless Miss Axhead saw the collection very soon she would become bogged down among her specials and we should never get an order at all. Miss Stallybrass sensed it too.

"I think it would be better if we showed you the collection and then we can put down the specials afterwards," she said in her fruitiest voice.

It was a tense moment. I knew that if Miss Axhead decided to deal with her specials first we were doomed.

"All right," she said, finally, after a long pause. "Only I must do my specials and time's getting on."

We showed the collection. Occasionally Miss Axhead spotted something that would do for a special and the proceedings ground to a halt while Miss Stallybrass hunted for suitable patterns. At the same time Miss Axhead was suggesting alterations.

"If you could use the collar of 'Dawn' and the back of 'Snowdrop' that would be just right for Mrs. Bean. Then you can do it the other way round for Mrs. Woodcock. They can't have the same style, their husbands belong to the same golf club. You remember Mrs. Bean. She's the one who . . ." Miss Axhead's voice sank to a whisper as she launched into blood-curdling details of the private life of the Beans.

"Special order 'Bean'," Miss Stallybrass wrote in her flowing hand. "Velour 477 Colour Ruby. Collar as Dawn. Back as Snowdrop. What size did you say Mrs. Bean is, Miss Axhead?"

"Ooh, she's a size!" said Miss Axhead, with relish. "I'll have to send you the measures. You'd better send me a sketch for Mrs. Bean and for Mrs. Woodcock, she's an awkward shape too. We like our pudding in the North." "Send

sketches," Miss Stallybrass wrote. I wondered how she was
going to cope with this one. "Dawn" and "Snowdrop" were
made by different tailors who detested one another.

At five o'clock the workrooms shut. There was a sound
like an avalanche as the girls thundered down the staircase
to the cellars where they kept their coats. Julie left, ostensibly
to catch a train. Bertha and Rosie remained. They looked as
displeased as they dared in the presence of Miss Stallybrass.

With maddening slowness the order was written down.
When it was complete it amounted to two thousand five
hundred pounds, but it was so peppered with codicils inserted
by Miss Axhead, all of which necessitated complex modifica-
tions of the original models, that it was doubtful if it could
ever be executed and still show a profit. A large part of it was
conditional on the dozens of "specials" being acceptable to
the Beans and the Woodcocks, most of whom appeared to
pass their time in playing a grown-up version of "I spy with
my little eye" whilst their husbands were on the golf course.

At six-forty-five Miss Axhead was taken into the office for
a final little drink with my parents. "It will be nice to have
a chat," she remarked as she rose from the settee, which
groaned as if in thankfulness at her departure. "I don't
think any of my girls realise what a hard job we have of
it."

"I entirely agree," said Miss Stallybrass. As always it was
impossible to tell what she was agreeing with.

"Are all our customers like Miss Axhead?" I asked Miss
Stallybrass when finally she had been taken away.

"Some of them are a damn sight worse," she replied
unexpectedly. "Poor old Mary Axhead. As well as that dear
little dog she's got a sister who's not very well."

"I didn't know you liked dogs," I said.

"Me!" she said. "I loathe 'em!"

"It wasn't a bad order," I said.

"Half of it won't be confirmed and she'll go around getting sketches and patterns from other suppliers for the specials before she makes up her mind. Most of them we shan't hear of again," said Miss Stallybrass.

There was a tense moment when the Head of the Costume Department, who had been waiting all day to intercept Miss Axhead, confronted Miss Stallybrass. Not only had she waited but she had been forced to accommodate Miss Stallybrass's other customers in her showroom, none of whom bought suits. She was justifiably incensed. She too was remunerated on a salary and commission basis.

"I'm awfully sorry, dear," said Miss Stallybrass, in a tone that showed that she was not really sorry. "But after all," smiling sweetly at her colleague who was quivering with barely suppressed fury, "it doesn't really matter, does it, as long as she puts down an order with one of us. It's all for the good of the firm."

In the succeeding weeks, from my vantage point in Miss Stallybrass's showroom, I saw the Buyers as they passed before me in a phantasmagoria of shapes and sizes and in their various sexes.

There were old, experienced Store Buyers as battered as sea captains, who knew exactly what they were going to buy before they even set eyes on the collection because they had been buying the same sort of things from us for twenty years. For them the fashion of a season had little significance. What they wanted was something to cover the nakedness of their well-hipped customers. Confronted with a coat with a hint of a current trend in it, something that was the pride and joy of the Model Workroom, they smiled knowingly at Miss Stallybrass and asked her for something "more sensible". The orders they placed could be calculated in advance to the nearest fifty pounds. It was lucky that this was so. They were the solid foundation of the business of Lane and Newby.

Then there were Central Buyers, who bought for great groups of stores instead of individual branches. They usually arrived with an assistant in tow to do the dirty work. They came armed with crocodile handbags like small portmanteaux and big black kalamazoo note-books in which the details of what they saw were noted down meticulously. Either this, or they completely ignored the collection and talked about some ancient wrong that had been done to them by Miss Stally-brass's predecessor ten years before the war. One male Buyer carried a slide-rule, presumably as a weapon of intimidation. Some of the men were invincibly rude, mistaking a show of ill-manners for business acumen. These Central Buyers were much-travelled. To my untutored imagination they seemed to offer the possibility of orders beyond the dreams of avarice, but I soon came to realise that so far as Lane and Newby were concerned this was a delusion. Even when the combined effort of Miss Stallybrass and Mr. Wilkins was successful in extracting an order from a Central Buyer it was so hemmed in by conditions and the terms which they offered were so cut-throat that it was scarcely possible to execute it and at the same time show a profit. Sometimes they insisted on a sample being produced in advance. Having accepted the sample, when the bulk of the order was ready for delivery they would contrive to discover some minute variations from the original which gave them the excuse to cancel the order in its entirety. They would then suggest taking delivery at an even lower price in order, as they put it, "to help us out".

In some stores the management had split the fashion departments into many sub-sections, under the impression that by so doing they were helping their customers. Then the Buyers were forced to travel about in a body, rather like a travelling circus, in the charge of a Fashion Co-ordinator, a strong-minded woman who acted as ringmaster. Her job was to make sure that they didn't all buy the same things. Confronted with a collection as modest as ours the Buyers of departments with arch-sounding titles—*Teen-age and Twenty, Not So Young* and *The Twilight Room*, sometimes took the easiest way out and bought nothing at all.

There were Buyers who were also proprietors. Most of them owned "Madam Shops". Often they were younger than the Store Buyers. They carried what seemed to be a large part of their stocks on their own backs and great wads of bank notes, which they thumbed impressively. Some Madams had been set up in business by admirers, preferring this tangible but precarious asset to the more conventional rewards. Madams could put down orders that would have been very welcome from store buyers, but as many of them only employed a book-keeper on a part-time basis, if at all, their financial stability was often open to question. The confirmation of the order meant little if, as Mr. Wilkins said, they were "rocky". Mr. Wilkins had a fine nose for a potential bankrupt. And there were Buyers from old established family businesses in the provinces. Sometimes they brought the entire family with them: the Proprietor, usually an elderly gentleman in a cheviot suit who knew my father; his wife, who nearly always wanted something for herself; the daughter, a kittenish creature in twin-set and pearls; and a son. Mostly the sons looked despairing and lost. None were as awful as young Mr. Fumble of Throttle and Fumble.

During these re-unions Miss Stallybrass and the Buyer exchanged significant glances while the proprietor and my father talked about old times and Mr. Wilkins, as suave and non-committal as ever, thumbed through the models on the rails, searching for something suitable for the wife. These customers from old-established businesses lent a certain humanity to the business of buying that was lacking in their more sophisticated counterparts from the cities. Many of them brought offerings of farm produce which were presented to my parents and Miss Stallybrass; a reminder that London in 1946 was still a beleaguered fortress.

More remote were the Buyers for "Export", a word currently fashionable that had even reached Lane and Newby, where it was regarded as one of the more harmless foibles of Sir Stafford Cripps. They arrived hot-foot off the boat from Dar-es-Salaam and Mombasa in company with agents whom they regarded with suspicion. They spoke of a way of life in the rarefied atmosphere of the African highlands which it was difficult to envisage in Great Marlborough Street. We were seldom able to satisfy them. Nothing made by Lane and Newby was washable.

Within these divisions there were Good Buyers; Dishonest Buyers, who expected presents in kind and whose orders were scaled precisely to the amount of entertainment they received; Mad Buyers, who gave enormous orders, perhaps as a form of emotional release and then cancelled them as soon as they returned home; Drunken Buyers with faces like beetroots; and Buyers with extra-mural interests. There were Buyers who took the *Reader's Digest*—Cultured Buyers; Buyers devoted to Buchmanism, with fixed smiles for everyone; Buyers devoted to cats, budgerigars, spiritualism, knitting. Their interests were legion. Most of them had had to fight to get where they were. Most were proud of the distance they had come, others were almost pathologically ashamed. And there were the Scottish Buyers, the most likeable of the lot, loyal to their suppliers and desperately underpaid.

CHAPTER ELEVEN

EXPORT OR DIE

OUR FAILURE to satisfy the Buyers from Africa did not go unnoticed by my father. Although he disapproved of the Government, faced with the alternative of exporting or going under he rose to the challenge. He wrote a long letter to the Board of Trade in which he said that Lane and Newby were anxious to participate in the export drive.

In reply he received a courteous letter telling him that everything possible would be done to assist him and a few days later an official from the Board of Trade arrived at Great Marlborough Street to find out whether our productions were exportable.

It was perhaps unfortunate that the man who was selected for this mission had only recently been transferred to the Board of Trade from the Ministry of Agriculture and Fisheries. He had spent most of his working life on statistical work connected with the processing of herring. It was not surprising that he knew nothing about women's clothes and he looked at Miss Stallybrass's productions with considerable awe.

"You can see for yourself that they are of excellent quality," my father said to him.

"That's what we want—quality," said the official, a Mr. Pocklington, eagerly taking the bait which was offered to him. "I was told to be particularly careful about the quality. Your goods seem, if I may say so, to be of particularly robust construction."

"Well, Mr. Newby," he said, rising from the show-room

settee still grasping his umbrella from which all attempts to separate him had proved futile. "I think you've got what we want—what the Country wants, I shall say as much to the Head of my Department when I make my report. Of course, you must realise that, so to speak, I am only the 'Deus ex Machina' but I don't think we shall encounter any difficulties."

"What about a cup of tea?" said my father who was himself longing for one.

The whole business of assessing the export-worthiness of Lane and Newby had taken far less time than Mr. Pocklington had bargained for. He had allocated the entire afternoon to his investigation. Loath to return to his uncomfortable office (he was not in a grade which entitled him to a carpet on the floor) he accepted gratefully. As a result he spent the rest of the afternoon in my father's office talking about the North Sea and fish, subjects which they both found more congenial than the export business.

"You know," said my father when Mr. Pocklington had left, "I found him a very decent sort of fellow. It's a pity they don't employ more of these out-door sort of chaps instead of all those whey-faced johnnies. He may not know much about fashion but at least he's the sort of man who gets things done. The sea teaches you to make decisions."

"I don't think he's ever been to sea," I said. "I thought I heard him say that he'd always been in an office."

"Men like that don't go around boasting about what they've done," he said. "That's why it's called 'The Silent Service'." Triumphantly, he looked at me over his glasses.

Mr. Pocklington was as good as his word. The name of Lane and Newby was added to a short list of particularly accommodating exporters which was then disseminated throughout the world by the Commercial Attachés and Secre-

taries in our Embassies and Consulates. Unfortunately whoever was responsible for drawing up the list forgot to specify
what commodities we were prepared to export and throughout
the eight years which I spent at Lane and Newby's we
received letters from the furthest-flung corners of the earth
asking us this very question. A surprising number of these
correspondents didn't even bother to ask what we dealt in.
They simply assumed that, like the Army and Navy Stores
before the war, we had everything. The requests poured in:
From Nome, where they were short of flannel shirts; Flagstaff,
Arizona, where they wanted parts for obsolescent motor cars;
Patagonia—sheep dip and umbrellas; Benares—brass water
pots for the tourist trade; Fulacuta and Bafata, two places I
had never heard of in Portuguese Guinea, alarm clocks and
contraceptives (the latter to be sent by surface mail in plain
envelopes); bicycles and blankets for places in the high Andes
with the unpronounceable names of Inca kings; uniforms for
the members of a brass band in a sultanate on the shores of
the Persian Gulf (the only people who seemed to want clothes).

Reading these letters was a fascinating experience. Quite
suddenly it seemed, 54, Great Marlborough Street had become
a shop window of the world. A world in which the laws of
supply and demand were temporarily suspended—the
suppliers having everything and the buyers nothing.

Nor were the terms particularly onerous. "I buy all things,
Good and Bad Qualities," one merchant, Raschid Ali, wrote
with refreshing candour, from Aden. "Therefore I think with
you we can do good businesses. Please rash me descriptions of
your merchandises, prices found on board ships and your best
quotations so that we may start our connections."

My father was delighted and replied to all these letter personally. Reluctant to sever the "connections" he had so unexpectedly made, he never actually told his correspondents

that he was not in a position to supply their needs. His replies always included a short homily on the advisability of only buying goods that were British made. Having raised their hopes in this way he then proceeded to deflate them.

"As a result of the efforts made by the Old Country in the late struggle," he wrote, "we now find that many essential materials are 'in short supply'. This shortage is likely to continue until such time as the present government is put out of office. Meanwhile . . ."

But although his letters must have mystified the recipients they did little to deter them. The majority, loath to return to the official letter writer in the market place replied with the same letter which they had sent originally; this being the only letter which they had at their disposal in English at any rate.

The letters were only the harbingers. Soon the merchants themselves began to arrive on our doorstep; a succession of picturesque foreigners all of whom had been drawn there by the magical efforts of Mr. Pocklington of the Board of Trade. Gathered together they would have made a picturesque group in their various national costumes. There were men from the Ivory Coast wrapped in gaily striped stuffs; enormous banias from Calcutta in mud-splashed dhoties; pock-marked men from Asia Minor in sad civilian suits; Indonesians in gorgeous silks and plastic raincoats, and a host of others. They had two things in common: none of them spoke English; all were blue with cold. Most travelled uneasily with their wives.

My father was in his element. He offered them tea and cake and barley water which most of them declined on religious grounds; promised them sketches and patterns and in certain cases, if he considered them sufficiently comely, even allowed the wives to buy coats "wholesale" from Miss Stallybrass "to keep the cold out". Outfitted by Miss Stallybrass they looked like peacocks served up at table with greens and boiled potatoes.

This open-handedness was unnecessary in the case of a furtive-looking Sikh who arrived carrying a suitcase to which he managed to transfer unseen a very expensive camel-hair coat at the same time as he was warmly praising the collection —a modern version of the Indian Rope Trick. No more was heard of the Sikh, or for that matter of any of the other visitors.

Another result of the patronage of the Board of Trade was that we suddenly found ourselves licensed to buy materials of a quality that we had believed to be extinct, that were reserved " for export only ". Although to the best of my know-ledge none of it was ever exported Mr. Wilkins and Miss Stallybrass were delighted and soon Miss Webb was busily engaged cutting it up for home consumption in the stockroom. As a result our home trade temporarily improved.

All this activity had a most beneficial effect on my father's health. When his old friends, the giants of the wholesale manufacturing business, met him in Margaret Street, in answer to their anxious enquiries about what he was doing about export (Haven't got enough for the home market, let alone for the exports, they used to say, offering him a huge Larranaga) my father would reply that he had as much export business as he could cope with and that it was developing strongly. As a result he found his reputation enhanced and he was asked to serve on a number of trade committees deal-ing with the problems of export.

CHAPTER TWELVE

SOMETHING WHOLESALE

Now that I seemed dedicated to the wholesale business whether I liked it or not, I began to take a more intelligent interest in the clothes we were producing.

During the war the fashion industry had had to rely almost entirely on native inspiration and what it could lift bodily from the pages of American Vogue. This was all very well while the war was still going on but in 1946 the results were alarmingly apparent even to someone as ignorant as I was. Unless they suffered from fallen arches most of the younger dressmakers had joined one or other of the women's services or had worked long hours in factories with their heads done up in white pudding cloths, making things that were far more lethal than anything they had dreamed up in their own workrooms. Some of the best tailors, but not the majority of course, had gone as far afield as Wales where, raised to the rank of Sergeant-Major, they had set up shadow factories in quarries and churned out battle dresses and shrouds for the duration, returning at war's end to bore stiff those who had stayed behind with stories of the perils they had undergone from falling slate.

It was not only within the island that simple patriotism had overcome commercial instinct. Across the Channel the French had been more than equal to the calls that had been made on them. In spite of terrible shortages, with the enemy on their doorsteps, they had put extra yards of material into their productions, "pour embarrasser les Boches", as they put it.

Women of fashion, bowed by the weight of gigantic pieces of millinery and garments which contained as much as two-and-a-half times the amount of stuff that had been required to make the same thing in 1939, were hurt to find their motives questioned by the liberators who found them pursuing a way of life that their propaganda had convinced them was impossible. Both sides were incensed.

In England the results were less ludicrous but extremely drab. With a few notable exceptions high fashion had become petrified in a cast that was a vague copy of military uniform. Ordinary clothes were even more ordinary than usual.

It was not long before I had the opportunity to see for myself what we ourselves were capable of at Lane and Newby. Apart from a really gorgeous trousseau of silk underclothes and nightdresses which had been made for her in a nunnery by fallen girls who were in process of being re-claimed by this odd form of occupational therapy, my wife had arrived in England with a very attenuated wardrobe. Foolishly, I had told her that she would be able to get whatever she needed "through the business".

"It's quite easy when you're actually in it," I boasted. "Much better quality in England." At this time my total experience of the business was made up of that disastrous visit to Sheffield, some abortive deep-breathing exercises with Lola below ground and the doubtful privilege of being able to say that I had cut up three-quarters of a mile of material, some of it wrongly.

"We'll fix her up with some clothes, dear," my mother said on the day following her "little talk" with Wanda. To this day I do not know what the "little talk" was about. My wife was as silent as the grave about it. Presumably it was to tell her that she had married a lunatic. "I'll speak to Miss

Stallybrass about it. We can make something special for her in the Model Workroom."

I was quite happy about this. I felt that if my mother was taking an interest nothing really disastrous could happen. She herself could take the most ghastly looking dress off the hook, put it on and by doing so turn it into a good dress. It was as if she conferred a benison on the thing by virtue of having touched it. In the Church a similar result is sometimes arrived at by the judicious sprinkling of holy water in some un-hallowed place.

But my mother and I were the victims of delusion. I failed to realise that her ability to turn a bad dress into a good one by the simple act of putting it on was nothing more than a piece of sleight-of-hand. She on her part should have known that it is almost impossible for anyone connected with the wholesale to get anything for themselves without suffering humiliation. To have "something special" is to invite real disaster. Perhaps this is the reason why some Savile Row tailors are so badly dressed that, having set eyes on them, prospective customers have been known to make for the door under the impression that they will be fitted out with some-thing similar. But they at least are paying the full price and their own inherent knowledge of what a suit should look like may save them from disaster. In the wholesale there is an unspoken thought that hovers constantly in the air that you are jolly lucky to be getting anything at all.

Wanda had an interview with Miss Stallybrass. It was not particularly reassuring. "An old woman came down and took my measures and said she knew what I needed. She was in a hurry. Miss Stallybrass said that she would send me some patterns. Everyone seemed very busy."

"That must have been Miss Fitchett," I said.

"She had little, what do you call them? *Baffi*?"

"Moustaches. That was Miss Fitchett. I only hope she knows what she's doing."

Weeks passed. The weather grew colder. In despair Wanda went off to Harrods and bought herself some warm clothes. Because we were in the wholesale, at Lane and Newby's we were showing clothes intended to be worn in the sort of summer that occurs in Britain only twice in a century. On Monday mornings before the antiquated heating arrangements got going Rosie and Julie, rooted from their looking glass, left vapour trails in the air as they went through their act, rigged out in the putty-coloured rayon shantung that Miss Stallybrass had decreed as being OK for Garden Parties in 1946, and their teeth chattered modishly like castanets. Only Bertha, with whom I was scarcely on speaking terms, more generously upholstered by mother nature, seemed impervious to the fearful cold. The following summer when for the first time since the end of the war the use of fur was permitted and we showed coats that were intended to be worn in the depths of winter, they all crawled about like displaced esquimaux. It was an odd business. Living always six months ahead of myself time soon ceased to have any meaning. At twenty-four, old age came zooming towards me.

Months passed. There was still no news of Wanda's "specials". When I mentioned them to Miss Stallybrass she laughed, said something about Rome not having been built in a day and made a note on her blotter. As she changed the blotting paper every day I was not confident that anything would come of it. I also spoke to my mother.

"It can't be long now," she said. "You must remember that I have very little control over Miss Stallybrass. It's just as difficult for me, dear. Besides, I thought Wanda had bought some clothes." Then suddenly, when the first crocuses were emerging suspiciously in the parks she was hailed to Great

Marlborough Street for a fitting. It seemed odd when she had
not even chosen the material.

She returned from it strangely silent. On her face was a
look that I had seen only once before; when we returned to
the village where her father and mother and their ancestors
before them had lived from time immemorial to find it burned
to the ground by the Germans. In the night great silent tears
rolled down her cheeks. I was very disturbed.

One evening I came home to find the drawing-room full of
tissue paper. There was no sign of Wanda. "Don't come in,"
she said from the bedroom. "I'm just putting my 'specials'
on." She gave the word a most sinister emphasis.

I waited. "You can come in now," she said. "Look what
they've done to me, your bloody firm."

At first I couldn't believe that it was my wife. She was
dressed in a wool georgette coat that was a purplish shade of
navy. The style was what is known in the trade as "edge-to-
edge"—that is to say it had straight fronts drawn together at
the waist by a pair of braid buttons that were like enormous
joke cuff-links. The shoulders, which were also enormous, were
absolutely square and must have been stuffed with several
pounds of wadding to produce such an effect. But it was the
sleeves that really compelled attention. From the shoulder to
the elbow they were narrow, below it they opened out like
the calyx of some monstrous flower. The cuffs had little points
which hung down forlornly. On the right breast someone had
stitched a little bunch of artificial snowdrops. It was the sort
of coat into which very, very old ladies are inserted by their
faithful maids on those occasions on which it is imperative
that they should be exposed to the public gaze.

"That's the coat," she said, flinging it on the floor. "And
don't you tell me that it's too big. I'm size 12. They told
me it was better to have it a bit bigger because I would prob-

ably put on weight and it would save an alteration. Now look at the dress ! " She burst into tears.

The dress was of the same material as the coat, only this time it was the colour called "wine". Whoever had dreamed up the ensemble must have thought that a cross-over bodice would make a nice contrast to the edge-to-edge coat, because it had a cross-over bodice. A cross-over bodice is mistakenly believed in the wholesale to be good for large sizes. The edges were trimmed with white piqué which showed up nicely against the dark red material. The skirt was the product of a really diabolical imagination. It had four separate sets of pleats in it, two at the front and two at the rear, presumably to allow the occupant to "get about" more easily. It was like a maternity dress for the wife of the oldest man in the world still living somewhere in the Anatolian highlands. I had never seen anything like it in my life.

"Good God ! " I said.

"Boo-Hoo ! " roared my wife. "And do you know what one of them said when they all stood round looking at me like a lot of crows? 'You know, Mrs. Eric, you're going to be a really distinguished-looking woman—when you're older.' And Miss Stallybrass said that she knew a wholesale place where I could get a nice hat that would be an exact match."

"I don't think they meant it like that," I said, without conviction. "Well you tell me what they did mean," she mooed. "I'm so unhappy (she pronounced it 'unhoppy') I want to go back to my country and my people. I wasn't rich but nobody treated me like this."

Later that night we took the whole dreadful outfit into the garden and set fire to it. There were a number of complaints from neighbours about the smell and it was an undoubted extravagance with millions starving in Europe but I felt that it was justified.

A few weeks later the head of the "Gown Department" suddenly died after years of faithful service and I persuaded my parents, much against their will, to put me in charge of it. I felt that in the circumstances it was the least that they could do.

CHAPTER THIRTEEN

HI! TAXI!

MY PARENTS' journey to Great Marlborough Street each morning was attended with some state. They used to travel from their house at Hammersmith Bridge by taxi, and always employed the same taxi-man for the run out and home. My mother insisted on the taxi because, she alleged, my father was too frail to travel by bus or train and my father used it reluctantly because he thought that public transport was too much for my mother. The real reason for this extravagance was that travelling with my father by any other means was such a nerve-shattering experience that no one who had undergone it was ever likely to repeat it.

In the course of five years the English had become a race who automatically formed queues for everything. It was not altogether a fault; in a world that was tumbling to pieces before their eyes it was the only way they knew of preserving their society from total anarchy. My father had failed to adapt himself to this new order; probably he had not even noticed that it had come to pass. Whatever the reason the results for anyone who was with him were extremely alarming.

"Here's a bus," he would say as we stood together in Oxford Street during the rush hour and, totally oblivious of a queue twenty yards long that had formed in the drizzle, he would launch himself on to the platform. The first time he did this I followed his example and was ordered off the bus by the conductor. My father was allowed to remain on board.

"Come on!" he shouted to me where I stood on the pavement in grave danger of being lynched, "there's plenty of room." No one said anything to him and as the bus drew away I saw a middle-aged lady offer him her seat. He arrived home half an hour before I did.

In his company a journey on foot was equally difficult. Like a man of the Rennaissance my father was constantly being overcome by the wonder of the world in which he lived. Walking down a street he would suddenly glimpse some odd cloud formation in the sky or a man with a goitrous protuberance close at hand and without warning he would stop in his tracks in order to enjoy the sight more closely. As a result the simplest excursion made by our family resembled a street-fighting patrol in hostile herritory. I would be some fifty yards ahead, still talking to my father, oblivious of what had happened; my mother would be lingering as innocuously as possible in the middle, waiting for my father to get going again; and my father would be somewhere down the street with his back to us looking at whatever had taken his fancy. My mother put it very neatly after one of these exhaustingly crablike excursions. "The trouble with your father," she said, " is that when I go out with him he always makes me feel like a street-walker."

This was the reason for the taxi. The taxi-man was called Mr. Walford. He was a real London cabbie of a type that is now almost extinct. His cab was of the same vintage, only the war had saved it from being condemned. It had buttoned upholstery; inside it was as dark as the grave. In the exposed position which he occupied in order to drive it Mr. Walford wore several overcoats, but this was only when he was actually at the wheel in inclement weather. When he called for my parents he was always exceptionally spruce in a snuff-coloured overcoat, a bowler hat and a cravat with a horseshoe pin in it.

He used to arrive at the house at Hammersmith Bridge, sound a prolonged blast on his horn and settle down to smoke his pipe with the flag of the meter still at " For Hire " whilst my father completed his toilet. This usually took about an hour, but Mr. Walford was never impatient and when finally my parents appeared, my mother elegant in furs and my father in a long tweed overcoat, he always gave them the same welcome. " Morning, Guvnor," he used to say in his hoarse voice, "Morning, Madam." In summertime he always wore a red rose in his buttonhole that came from his garden and before they set off he always presented one to my mother too.

I think that this was the only time in his stormy acquaintance with the internal combustion engine that my father was really content to be driven by somebody else. If anyone could be, Mr. Walford was the ideal driver for my father. He made the same sort of noises at other road users that my father would have made if he had himself been at the wheel.

" GRRRRRRR. Look where you're going, can't you ! " he used to shout at some luckless motorist who had the temerity to come abreast of him, causing the offender to swerve violently.

" You're quite right. Chaps like that shouldn't be allowed on the road at all," my father said in corroboration. " SILLY KITE ! " he shouted, putting his head out of the window and glaring at the cause of the trouble who by this time was beginning to believe that he really had done something wrong.

So that he could carry on a running conversation with Mr. Walford my father always left the window open between the front and rear compartments, but as both of them were a little hard of hearing they were forced to shout at the tops of their voices. The din they made added to the discomfort of my mother who was already freezing in the draught produced by the open window.

On arrival at Great Marlborough Street the descent from the taxi was always accompanied by a good deal of ceremony, so much so that passers-by usually stopped to find out what was going on; but finally my parents arrived safely in the hall, the doorbell pinged behind them and, as they stood there trailing rugs and scarves, Miss Gatling would emerge from the Counting House and before they had even the chance to take their coats off would pour into their ears the news of some fresh disaster that was threatening the business. It was unfortunate that although what she said had always a sound foundation of truth the moment at which she chose to impart it was so inopportune that my parents took very little notice.

In the evening the whole process took place again; only by this time Mr. Walford was anxious to get home to his supper and my parents had had enough too. I never found out how Mr. Walford managed to find himself in the neighbourhood of Great Marlborough Street at six-thirty every evening but he always contrived to, except on the occasions when he "broke down". Sometimes he broke down with my parents inside. On one occasion my father prevailed on Mr. Walford to open the back of the taxi by lowering the hood so that he could enjoy a "good blow" on the way home. The mechanism by which the hood was lowered had not been used since before the war and once the hood was lowered no power on earth was able to shut it again. As a result of his love of fresh air the taxi was out of action in Mr. Walford's "garridge" where for two days the hood successfully resisted the combined efforts of the staff to close it.

Sometimes I was in such a state of penury that I too accepted a lift to Hammersmith Bridge in the taxi, but this was seldom a success. By the evening my father was usually rather grumpy and the journey resolved itself into a gloomy post-mortem on the events of the day with particular reference to my own shortcomings.

My father was a member of something in the City called the Guild of Freemen. I never really knew what it was, but the Guild used expensive writing paper for its correspondence and my father possessed a parchment scroll on which he was referred to as being "Trusty and Well-Beloved". Each year the Guild of Freemen met together for a great beano in the Guildhall, a banquet of many courses at which toasts were drunk. At the culmination of the evening the Archbishop of Canterbury made a speech.

One morning I found my father mulling over some impressive-looking invitations in his office.

"The Guild of Freemen is having its banquet in a couple of weeks time," he said. "I thought we might all go. It will give you a chance to wear your decoration." He smiled at me disarmingly.

On the night of the banquet we assembled at my father's house. Wanda and my mother were dressed in the splendid stuffs that are appropriate to such an occasion and I was wearing my father's second-best suit of tails; a suit that had been made for him in 1895 by a tailor in Maddox Street with trousers that fitted as closely as a glove. That my father should have permitted himself a second suit of tails was a measure of the original suit's dilapidation. We made a festive picture. Although we did not realise it, it was the last time that we should do so.

"I thought we'd have a bottle of wine," said my father, "'28 Bollinger. It should be cold enough. I brought it home in old Walford's cab," he added mischievously. "Sometimes they don't give you much to drink at these sort of do's."

I was surprised to hear him say this, but my father had

attended so many dinners in the City in his life-time that I
did not contradict him.

He had hired a car to take us to the Guildhall. It was a
pleasant journey. My father was in good spirits and made us
all laugh.

At the Guildhall, where we arrived a bare five minutes
before the banquet was due to begin, the women disappeared.
My father and I were left at the foot of a staircase where two
flunkeys were ladling something into glasses from an enormous
urn.

"That smells good," said my father, sniffing appreciatively.
"Punch," said one of the men with a hint of reproof in
his voice as if my father should have known what it was.
"Well, let's have some!" said my father.

We were each given a glass of something strong and
sweetish that seemed to have a basis of rum. After the Bollinger the effect was unpleasant.

As we took our seats in the Banqueting Hall my father
turned to the waiter who was standing behind his seat and
handed him something. "Just look after my son and I," I
heard him say, giving the man a wink.

"I'll look after you, Sir," the waiter said. He was a sat-
urnine-looking fellow, a little like Frognall the commissionaire
at Throttle and Fumble.

The dinner began.

There was grace and soup and sherry and more sherry and
fish and Moselle and an entrée and claret and I think there was
some sort of sweet, rather dank, and port and innumerable
toasts. And because my father had given the waiter something
to encourage him to look after us there was twice as much to
drink for us as there was for everyone else, including the
Archbishop.

With the pressure on I soon found that I had a nervous

compulsion to drink whatever was put in front of me. No sooner had I tasted a wine than a great hand in a white cotton glove appeared over my shoulder and refilled the glass. By the time the port arrived I was stupendously drunk. My father was drunk too, but because of his age and his silver hair, the fact that his head was sunk on his chest and he was ostensibly asleep made him less an object of remark than I was. As if to belie his condition indeed he suddenly roused himself in his chair and said in a loud voice to no one in particular, "Very warm. Must get some fresh air," and incontinently left the room.

"My Lords, Ladies and Gentlemen. Pray silence for His Grace, The Archbishop of Canterbury." It was the toastmaster. To me he looked like a great, boiled lobster. As his Grace rose to speak I realised that I was going to be sick.

I too, rose; mumbled something to the woman on my left, saw through a haze a line of scandalised faces and made for the nearest exit. The door was guarded by two footmen in breeches and silk stockings. They had calves like Miss Axheads'. I pushed past them through the door and was immediately sick. To my surprise I found myself not disgracing myself as I imagined I would be in front of a lot of chauffeurs in an anteroom but alone in the open air under the stars. I was in a bombed transept of the Guildhall and I was standing on a wooden cat-walk erected by workmen over what must have been the ground floor and the cellars of the building. The hole, for that is what it was, seemed very deep. It was surrounded by a high, medieval-looking wall. There was not a door or window to be seen. I was trapped.

My appearance was now so disgusting that I could not go back and take my seat with the other diners even if I had been capable of doing so. The only thing to do was to climb the wall, which was not difficult. I wondered what had happened to my father. He was far less agile than I was. I felt too ill to think about the agonies that our wives were suffering, abandoned by two drunks in the presence of an Archbishop of Canterbury.

From the top of the wall I looked down twenty feet into a City street. I commended myself to God and dropped.

I landed at the feet of a policeman, who shone his torch on me and regarded me with interest.

"I've just been to the Dinner," I said with as much dignity as I could muster. "The one with the Archbishop of Canterbury."

"If you take my advice you'll cut off home," he said, not unkindly. A cab was passing and he signalled to it.

"Hammersmith Bridge," I said.

"Outside the limit," said the driver. I told him I didn't mind what it cost. All the way home in the cab I was sick out of the window. The taxi-man made me clean it. As I was sluicing it down with buckets of water another cab appeared with my father in it. He too was leaning out of the window.

Although he was in a similar condition to myself, no longer drunk, unlike me he was not at all contrite.

"I can't imagine what they gave us to drink at dinner," he said, self-righteously, as I poured a bucket of water over his taxi. "This is what comes of drinking a lot of jobbed-up stuff on top of a bottle of good wine. Never put a beggar on a gentleman, that's what I say!"

CHAPTER FOURTEEN

A NICE BIT OF CRÊPE

" There was nothing basically new in the latest
London Designers Collection for Export . . .
Very little handling of new colour . . .
One inch drop in the hemline."

British Vogue. September 1946

I ASSEMBLED MY first collection in the Autumn of 1946.
It would be an exaggeration to say that I designed it; rather
I found myself swept away by events like a man heading for
Niagara Falls in a barrel while grizzled spectators offered
advice from the bank. I was the convener; the nodal point of
activity; Macbeth on the blasted heath without whose presence
the ghastly apparitions that I was to see in the succeeding
weeks would have no occasion to rear their heads.

The Collection I was about to make could scarcely be described as something that would shake the world. No newspaper, however desperate for news, would ever report it and
no one but wholesale customers would ever see it in its
entirety.

Day after day in the dog-days of Summer we sat in the
showroom—my mother, the Head of the Model Workroom,
and Kathie, the Stock keeper, whose job was the counterpart
of Miss Webb's in Coats, and me—while the representatives of
the silk and cloth houses with which we did business laid
before us swatches of the stuffs from which the collection was
to be made.

It was an exacting business. I soon learned the dangers of
choosing materials simply because I liked the design, without

first considering for what purpose I was intending to use them.

"I like that. Do you like it? "

"Yes, I like it."

"I think I like it. What are those things on it, cabbage roses? "

"They look like Brussel sprouts to me."

"But what's it for? "

"Let's pass it."

"Now I like that. You can use it on the cross."

"You can only use it on the cross."

"What sort of dress do you think? "

"I think it's cocktail. I can see it as a cocktail with a big bow at the back."

"Let's keep off bows, for God's sake."

"Don't say 'God', dear."

"What do you think of it, Kathie? "

"We had something just like it from Mr. Flukes last year, Mrs. Newby. It came in very late and it was all flawed. I shouldn't be surprised if this was left-overs."

"Ha-Ha, Miss Ingles! You will have your little joke. This is Swiss and very exclusive."

"In that case we'll be lucky if it ever arrives," said Kathie, gloomily.

"Let's pass it," said my mother. I was delighted.

"You're making a mistake," said Mr. Flukes. He didn't say as I expected him to, that we were making a mistake if we didn't mind him saying so.

Most of the representatives of the larger firms were men of military appearance. Because the business they were in made it easy for them to evade the sumptuary laws then in force, they appeared almost unnaturally spruce in contrast to the rest of the population. Almost to a man they were dressed in

Savile Row suits which they had acquired without coupons. Some wore ferocious moustaches and bowler hats which they wore tilted over their noses like officers of the Brigade of Guards in civilian dress.

The horrors of war seemed to have had surprisingly little effect on them. These men were not purged by what they had seen. Far from having learned humility they brought to their work a brusqueness that would be unthinkable today, for they were in the happy position of being able to sell anything however unseemly and any reluctance we displayed brought a reminder that what was being offered was on a quota, with the implication that we were lucky to be getting anything. During these séances one of them whom I particularly detested use to refer to me in asides to my mother as "The Boy".

In the midst of his multifarious activities my father always found time to appear on the scene to find out what we were up to. When he did so he showed a taste and acumen that were extremely acute, at variance with the conception of Olympian detachment which I had of him and, although a pretence of disagreement was made while he was present, as soon as he had left the room we usually confirmed his judgement by ordering the materials which he had admired.

These were the circumstances in which I set to work. Without really knowing what I was up to I decided that whatever else was made there was going to be a number of dresses which were not trimmed with little bows, decorated with beads or disfigured with drawn-thread work.

It was easy enough to control the Model Workroom. The decease of my predecessor, Miss Nuthall, had brought about a change in the leadership of the Model Workroom. The new incumbent who had herself started at the bottom as a junior was far more lively. She too was longing to make more exciting clothes and, in the same way as Miss Stallybrass and Mr. Wilkins, together we would have been a dangerous combination if only there had been any exciting clothes to inspire us; but unfortunately for us the world of fashion had ground to a standstill. In the Autumn collections made by the London Couture Houses there was little that was new. The colours were uninspiring and the hemlines fell one inch. The very sound of such a fall was like a knell, as if the lights were going out over Europe at the very moment when they were in process of being re-lit.

In the Wholesale, coats and suits still had square shoulders. Sometimes they were dropped shoulders with yokes which gave the wearer the appearance of having been decapitated by someone in a hurry who had trimmed down the neck and stuck the head back on again. Jackets were very long. Sometimes they had cut-away fronts, in which case they were called "Regency". Hats were jaunty in a mannish way. It was an Amazonian time.

Evening dresses, like the gatherings at which they were intended to be worn, were dispirited. The most popular material was crêpe of which there seemed to be inexhaustible supplies in shades of beige and "natural" or something hybrid that was called "greige".

Shoes had sling backs and open ends through which the toes protruded coyly like thumbs. The style was called "Peek-a-Boo". It was inappropriate as, apart from the design they were constructed as robustly as if the wearer was liable to be recalled to active service at any moment. Simple, unadorned court shoes were almost impossible to find. Perhaps no one wanted them—there is nothing easier than being knowing about fashion a decade after it has passed away.

For inspiration in making my collection I used the French, English and American Editions of Vogue; Harpers; L'Officiel, a remarkable magazine that was and still is a poor man's guide to the French Collections; pirated toiles purveyed by sinister little men with "connections" in Paris; and my own native wit such as it was. The result was an unholy brew which was watered down and made "more sensible" as my mother put it. It was fortunate that she intervened, otherwise the dress department might have come to a swifter end than it did.

As well as the regular staff we also employed outworkers who, now that the workrooms on the upper floors had been destroyed, (they went up in smoke in 1944) were responsible for the greater part of the production. The outworkers were elderly ladies who had been working for us exclusively, so far as we knew, for years. Most of them lived in distant suburbs. Together they constituted a remarkable secret army. Some were capable of really beautiful work and to these we entrusted the making of prototypes from sketches and toiles; others who were unimaginative or emotionally unstable were only given the repeat orders. One or two insisted on making their own models. They were the most difficult to deal with; freelance in the worst sense of the word, they constituted the Achilles heel of Lane and Newby.

One of the most atrocious was a Mrs. Ribble who had a workroom in uncharted country on the south side of the river, somewhere in the neighbourhood of London Bridge. No member of the firm had ever succeeded in finding it except my father and Brandon the porter who was sent there on some errand. On his return he had been interrogated as to what he had seen but all that could be got out of him was that it was "a mucky old place". My father was even less successful. He encountered Mrs. Ribble on the doorstep and as she showed no signs of inviting him in he had been forced to carry on a long conversation with her over a row of dustbins. Whatever secrets Mrs. Ribble's workroom concealed it seemed that they were not of a kind that she was willing to share with the world.

Less than a week before the collection was due to be shown she presented herself at Great Marlborough Street and demanded a large number of sample lengths. This was the first time I had actually seen Mrs. Ribble.

"Just give me some crêpe, dear," she croaked. "Paris says it's going to be crêpe. Crêpe and pleats." She was a woman of indeterminate age, something between fifty and seventy, with fingers so heavily ringed that they gave her the appearance of being armed with jewelled knuckle-dusters.

"But what are you going to make?"

"Don't you worry what I'm going to make," she said. "I know what you want. Something for Formal Wear. Something for the Evening Do's. I've been making them since before you were born."

I went to consult my mother. She was heavily engaged with a stolid, impassive woman called Mrs. Arbuthnot who looked exactly like a black beetle. For years Mrs. Arbuthnot had been making two-pieces for us. Every year she made exactly the same shape, apart from some minor variation, and every season it was as if she had never worked for us before in the whole of her life.

"This is what I want but with the seam here," my mother was saying.

"Couldn't make that, Mrs. Newby," Mrs. Arbuthnot said, pursing her lips. "My girls wouldn't stand for it."

"But, Mrs. Arbuthnot, 'Newmarket' was exactly the same except for the channel seaming."

"'Newmarket' didn't pay," said Mrs. Arbuthnot.

I took my mother to one side.

"There's a Mrs. Ribble in the showroom. She wants some sample lengths. She looks a terror to me."

"Miss Nuthall always used her. She makes evening dresses. Sometimes they're all right but she's very erratic. It's not very clean work but if you get a couple of styles from her that sell she's very useful, especially early in the season. Mason's wives seem to like them. The great thing is not to give her too much at once. Don't give her much at all."

Mrs. Arbuthnot was showing every sign of striking her tent and leaving.

"You haven't left her alone in the showroom, have you?"

"No, Yvonne's there. Why?"

"If you leave Mrs. Ribble alone with your new models for five minutes they'll be in Oxford Street in a week. Now, Mrs. Arbuthnot, as I was saying, it really isn't difficult. All you have to do is . . ."

"That's right, dear, give me a nice selection," said Mrs. Ribble when I returned to the showroom. "Nice pastels and some jewel colours—and Paris says beige."

When I told Kathie to give Mrs. Ribble half a dozen lengths of crêpe all she said was "Huh!"

After Mrs. Ribble had gone she came into the showroom.

"If I was you I shouldn't have given Mrs. Ribble all those delicate colours," she said. "Last time she brought in samples they were all covered with food and oil. She's got very dirty habits, Mrs. Ribble."

"Well, why didn't you say so before?"

"You're the boss," said Kathie, darkly.

It was now that my father showed himself possessed of a clairvoyant power that was lacking in the rest of us.

"Quite nice," he said when I showed him some of the new models from the workroom. "But they're not sellers. People don't come to us for that sort of thing. It's neither fish nor fowl. The Jews do them cheaper and almost as well. Let me see the costings.

"I should scrap those three," he said. "Sell 'em to a Madam Shop. Put a hundred per cent mark up on 'em. Get rid of 'em!"

"But they're the best of the lot."

"It doesn't matter. This isn't a Couture House. Where are you proposing to get the repeats made? We've only got two workers who can handle this kind of thing and they only turn out three dresses a week."

"I thought of making them in the Workroom. Doris says she can do them."

"Of course she can do them but what's she going to charge for them?"

"She says she'll do them at a special price."

"I expect she will," said my father. "It isn't her business and it isn't her money. Do you know what the Workroom means by a special price? It's twice what we have to pay anyone else for the same thing. The only way to make the Workroom pay is to give it all your specials and charge a thumping price for 'em. That's the only way to pay the wages. Have you looked at the wages book lately? Have a look at it. Those three dresses were toiles, weren't they? Put those into the costings as well and you'll find that you've priced yourself out of the market."

What followed I found even more depressing.

"I think you've made far too large a collection," he said. "It happens every season. I was always telling Miss Nuthall but she never listened. Women in this business are like prima-donnas. However many dresses you make you'll never have a perfect collection. There's always something you need later on. It's always better to wait and see which way the wind's blowing. You can always make more.

"Besides, there's something up this Autumn. Fashion's on the change. I had a letter from Madam Havet in Paris. She says that things have been at a standstill for so long that something's bound to happen in the Spring. She says that the hemline will 'descendre par l'escalier'."

He spoke of an ancient couturière, now almost blind, who occupied premises in the Place Vendôme. He had sent me to her a few weeks before with a letter of introduction. It said something for the memories it invoked that when the directrice read it to Madam Havet who was sitting on a sort of throne she had not only admitted me to the showing of the collection without payment but at the end of it she had allowed me to choose one toile for nothing. "For the past and for the future." This is the only time I ever received something for nothing in France and I have never heard of it happening to anyone else.

"I remember something similar after the first war," my father continued. "Everyone wanted gaberdine. We had thousands of yards of the stuff—then poof—we couldn't give it away. We had to job it all at a couple of shillings a yard. Then the hemlines went up and we were in trouble again.

"I see that you and your mother have put down some quite large orders for materials, especially with —— Textiles. I think you should cut them down."

"I don't think we can cut them down," I said. "You remember what that fellow Calverley-Smith was telling us. 'If you don't put them down now you won't get them at all.' You were in the room at the time."

"I'll go and see them," said my father, brightening at the thought of action. "I know old Brown."

He was as good as his word. Not only did he go and see old Brown and succeed in reducing the orders but he managed to extract a promise from him that he would reserve for us the same amount of material that we had originally ordered.

It was a triumph. I asked him how he had managed it.

"I've known old Brown for years," he said. "We used to row together. We were at Marlow in '94. I think it was '94. I was stroke. He rowed bow. I took him to the Café Royal and we had a jolly good yarn. I paid for the lunch and he stood me a very nice bottle of Burgundy.

"I wish I could keep Miss Stallybrass in order," he said. "She's put down a shocking order with . . . . . But they're a difficult lot. Of French extraction. Mingy. You have to get up early to deal with them. I've managed to cut it by half but that's still not enough. She's a chancer," he said.

"How did you do it?"

"I told them that they might not get their money."

"Is it true?" The very thought gave me a cold feeling in the stomach.

"It will be if we go on at this rate," my father said.

Gradually the collection evolved. The making of it was like every other from the humblest to the most grandiose. An air of insanity pervaded the building. Materials failed to arrive, came in lengths too short to make anything but a woollen comforter, got stuck in the Customs, or were such a miserable parody of what had been originally ordered that Kathie sent them back to the manufacturers. When they did arrive intact and without flaws we ourselves proceeded to maltreat them. Expensive stuffs were singed by the pleaters or else lost their colour in the process and were the subject of litigation. Embroideries were executed in shiny silk thread instead of being matt. Belts arrived in the wrong sizes or came back covered in glue, or were irretrievably lost. The matcher left a piece of precious French lace from Dognin on top of a bus when returning with it from a dye works in Ilford. The Workroom was decimated by an unseasonable outbreak of influenza.

To me, paradoxical as it may seem, the most peaceful place of all during this period of gestation was our own workroom. It was high up at the back of the house and it had a glass roof like a conservatory. Here the cold, northern light cast no shadow. It was very quiet and at night when the girls had gone home and the stands with the models on them were covered with dust sheets the place had a ghostly quality like an illustration by Leech in the Ingoldsby Legends. Only the postcards on the cupboard doors with love from Flo at Worthing, and Lily at Skegness, and the pin-ups of Alan Ladd and Bing gave it an air of homeliness.

This quietness persisted during the day. Here there was no worker's playtime. No radio on the go as there was at Mr. Grunbaum's and Mrs. Ribble's. The girls worked in silence or else talked in undertones and it seemed to me, watching them, that with their quiet withdrawn expressions they resembled, old and young, the twelfth-century sculptures of Antelami which I had seen once in the Baptistery at Parma. The concentration which they gave to their work gave to them too a kind of beauty which they would not have had if they had been typists or shop assistants. Perhaps it was because this was what they wanted to do. Certainly they could have earned more in a factory. Yet when it was five-thirty and time to go they rushed and bustled down the scrubbed wooden staircase and in the street became ordinary girls once more at whom the van boys whistled or else forbidding matrons in velour coats with shopping bags making for the bus.

The Outworkers were my greatest preoccupation. They took their sample lengths and vanished into thin air. They were in no hurry. They had plenty of work on hand, for they were still making "specials" for long-suffering customers from the previous season. Most of them were not on the telephone and they ignored postcards. It was only by making arduous journeys to Clapham, Peckham Rye and into the marsh lands of Kent and Essex that I managed to assemble the fruits of their labours.

In spite of the new sketches with which they had been provided and many hours of painstaking briefing, all the models which the outworkers produced were, with minute variations, exactly the same as those they had made for the last thirty years with the same amount of beading and drawn-thread work and this was regarded by everyone except myself as being highly satisfactory.

And there was Mrs. Ribble. Within three days of being issued with the materials she was back with the new samples. She arrived with a huge, tent-like bundle constructed from old bed sheets in which they were concealed. She had made six full-length dinner dresses with sleeves in sizes that ranged from 44 to 48. Basically they were all the same. The only variation was in the way in which the skirts were pleated and in the designs of the sequin embroideries. There was no question of fitting as they were already finished; in any event we had no one on the premises whom they would have fitted.

To my unaccustomed eye they were all equally frightful.

"Lovely, aren't they dear?" said Mrs. Ribble breathing heavily on me. She had been eating garlic. "This is what you want. Nice supple line. Nice drapery. Perhaps your little girl will put them on."

My assistant in the Gown Department was a girl called Yvonne. Yvonne put them on. The effect was overpowering. In Mrs. Ribble's size 44 which was cut with an unnecessary amplitude she looked infinitely lost and forlorn, like a parcel done up in yards and yards of crêpe-paper that had lost its string.

"Lovely," said Mrs. Ribble. "Look at the bugle beading. Just right for a Do."

"Mrs. Ribble," I said. "Why on earth did you make them all in such large sizes?"

"Why did I make 'em in such large sizes? That's a damn silly question. So you can mark 'em off, of course. Show 'em in the hand. Mark 'em off quick soon as you've got an order and I'll make a replacement. Robins' is already repeating."

"Do you mean that these dresses are already on sale?"

"Not these dresses, Mr. Newby, other dresses. You don't think I'd sell your dresses to Robins' do you? If you think that Mr. Newby all I can say is I'm very very sorry. I make all my dresses different. These are exclusive to Lane and Newby."

"But I can't mark this one off. It's got marks all over the skirt. It looks like gravy."

"Gravy," said Mrs. Ribble. For the first time she sounded really affronted. "I can't see any gravy. All my girls are very dainty with their work. I never allow food in the workroom."

"And this one's got oil on it."

"Where's it got oil on it? Show me the oil on it." She made a great business of examining the garment, holding it so close to her eyes that it would have been impossible for her to see anything at all. "Why those are just little marks. I can get those out in a moment."

"Well, get 'em out!"

"I didn't bring these dresses for you to pick holes in them you know," said Mrs. Ribble.

Two hours later they were back. So far as I could see nothing whatever had been done to them. After unsuccessfully disputing Mrs. Ribble's bill I abandoned the struggle. There was no time left to do anything else.

CHAPTER FIFTEEN

NORTH WITH MR. WILKINS

"NOW THAT you have your own department I think you should go North with Wilkins," said my father. "He's going on The Journey. I'll speak to him about it. He makes all the arrangements."

I was filled with foreboding. The Spring Collection was almost ready. By now I knew enough about myself to realise that so far as Lane and Newby's was concerned I was what would be described in current jargon as "accident prone". Anything I touched, however innocuous it seemed, became a travesty of its original nature. It was as if I carried with me the seeds of spectacular disaster which, unknowingly, I sowed broadcast and which shot up as monstrous growths to confront me. I felt like a witch doctor whose mumbo-jumbo worked.

The Journey took place twice a year. It was the visit to Sheffield on a grand scale. It lasted ten days to a fortnight. The timing of it was all-important. If it was made a week too early the Buyers had not received their buying allowance and if it was a week too late then they had spent it all. Anyone who made The Journey spoke of it with awe. Now that the Manager of the Gown Department was no more, the only survivors still in the business were my parents and Mr. Wilkins.

Listening to them as they reminisced about it, unconscious of the impression they were making, it seemed to me that the physical qualities needed were similar to those demanded of a competitor in the Modern Pentathlon, that gruelling Olympic event in which the participants ride horseback over a course littered with obstacles, fire pistols on an open range, fence, swim 300 metres in four minutes and run a cross-country— all in the space of five days.

It was not only physically exacting. The Journey also made considerable demands on the intellect. Exceptional adroitness was needed in answering leading questions. While it was impossible to give a truthful answer to most of them, it was equally disastrous to be detected in an actual falsehood as this would give an impression of moral instability.

There was a precise ritual connected with The Journey, in which future generations of savants may find as much significance as did the author of *The Golden Bough* in the slaying of the Priests at Nemi. It always began in the North with a visit to Glasgow and Edinburgh. The order in which they were visited was of no importance; it was impossible to do good business in both places. If the orders were large in Edinburgh then the Buyers in Glasgow were informed by some sort of bush-telegraph; the age-old animosity that exists between the inhabitants asserted itself and the orders were scaled down proportionately. If Glasgow was visited first then the same supernatural law operated, but in reverse. On one occasion my parents, in an endeavour to break this seemingly immutable sequence of events, changed their destination from Edinburgh to Glasgow at the last moment. They got no orders in either city. This happened before the war. It was now no longer possible to change one's destination at the last moment; accommodation was "in short supply" and had to be booked months in advance.

Using Glasgow and Edinburgh as bases, daylight raids could be made into the hinterland: to Dundee, Stirling, Perth and into the Lowlands; to Ayr, Peebles and Berwick-on-Tweed.

Travelling "light", with only a few of the best models, it was possible to reach Aberdeen, but the further the traveller got from his base the more the human spirit failed. Mr. Wilkins claimed that on one occasion he had reached Inverness, but no one at Lane and Newby's really believed him. If he did get there all he managed to do was to "introduce himself" as he put it. My mother always maintained that he did it by telephone.

South of the Border the journey took in Newcastle, Manchester, Liverpool and the great industrial heart of England, at which, wreathed in the smoke and flames of a thousand blast furnaces, Miss Trumpet, of Throttle and Fumble of Sheffield, stood guard like some ravening Fury at the mouth of Hell.

This was The Journey. It petered out undramatically in the Midlands with a visit to Nottingham. Nothing else was worth doing, at least on this scale. Wales, as my father said with a degree of historic truth, was "another problem". The Eastern Counties seemed purged of the thought of luxury by the winds that droned over them from the Ural mountains. The South Coast was so close to London that the Buyers went there anyway. In the West business was virtually non-existent, the further one travelled towards the setting sun the softer the air grew until in Devon and Somerset it was like trying to force one's way through cotton wool. Decisions that were matters of a moment in the North, in Bath and Torquay were drawn out intolerably. Beyond the River Tamar, in Cornwall, commerce petered out completely; cream teas and the decoration of wooden objects with red-hot pokerwork entirely absorbed the inhabitants. "No money in it," said Mr. Wilkins. He was quite right. The Journey was extremely expensive and the margin between success and financial failure was a hair's-breadth.

I now had to decide which dresses to take with me. It was a difficult problem. My father had been at considerable pains to brief me on the tastes of the Buyers whom I would encounter. They seemed to range from a degree of terrifying sophistication to one of extreme barbarism. I felt like the Swiss Family Robinson who, having landed on an alien shore with the materials for spending a night in the open, returned day after day to the wreck for objects which they might conceivably need in the future. In the end I took everything—even the hideous productions of Mrs. Ribble, which I felt should have been consigned to an incinerator.

In the last hours before our departure I found myself divorced from all responsibility. I was being prepared for the sacrifice. Set apart, as if in a dream, I watched the listing of the dresses (at cost price for insurance purposes) and the packing of them as Yvonne laid them one by one in three cabin trunks, swathed in reams of tissue paper. The space that was left was filled with order books, patterns and collapsible cardboard boxes which it was intended that I should use when calling on recalcitrant customers or potential ones who refused to visit the hotel. To me it seemed impossible that the results of so much toil and tribulation could be compressed into such a small space.

In his own department Mr. Wilkins was busy with the coats and suits. Before the war the heavy clothes had travelled in things called "coffins", vast, black oblong boxes like sarcophagae, in which they hung uncreased. They were so heavy that no post-war porter would handle them. They now stood mouldering in serried ranks in the cellars, giving them something of the air of a crypt.

I drew my "expenses" from Miss Gatling, but the pleasure of handling numbers of five-pound notes was swiftly dissipated.

She was at considerable pains to point out that the whole venture was wildly profligate and that in her opinion my inclusion in it was a complete waste of money. It was difficult not to agree with her.

These pleasantries were reserved for me; confronted with the stare of Mr. Wilkins, as bland as that of a confidence trickster on board the *Mauretania*, she was strangely silent.

The reason for this was that in the course of the last fortnight a chink had shown itself in Miss Gatling's seemingly impenetrable plate of proof, and Mr. Wilkins knew of it. I knew of it too. It had become apparent when my father decided that the letter headings on the firm's stationery were in need of modernisation.

"I think we must change our style," he said. "We can't go on talking about Mantles and Costumiers. There was a very decent young fellow here the other day, a representative from a printing firm. He showed me a lot of headings. Some of them were very agreeable. I don't want to give our customers the impression that we're stick-in-the-mud. I said I'd look into it. He was very keen on rowing. Belongs to Twickenham."

With his usual enthusiasm my father looked into it. What he found was not very pleasing. In the cellars, secreted in the coffins which they entirely filled were box upon box of stationery of all kinds: writing paper, invoices, statements, memorandum books, credit notes and all the other paraphernalia of business communication. At the most conservative estimate there was sufficient to last Lane and Newby for five years. The whole lot was stamped in the old way with "Mantle Manufacturers and Wholesale Costumiers" and a telephone number that was already extinct. This was the work of one of Miss Gatling's minions who in the midst of some acute paper shortage had been prevailed upon to place this gargantuan order on the grounds that printing was cheaper in quantity. While the knowledge of this mistake filled Mr. Wilkins and Miss Stallybrass with glee the only result, so far as I was concerned, was to plunge me into even greater melancholy. If this was the rate at which the modernisation of the firm was to proceed then it seemed unlikely that any of us would live to witness its conclusion.

Just before we left I had a final meeting with my father in his office.

"Wilkins has written to the Scottish customers," he said. "And he's got the tickets. You must have a good night's sleep, otherwise you'll be good-for-nothing tomorrow morning. I told him to book sleepers well in advance. Most of them are reserved for The Ministries. (He pronounced the words as though they were anathema.) Most of the time they never use 'em. Have a decent meal at night when you're finished. You can get a steak in the Grill Room at the North British—or you used to be able to before the War. I remember they used to have quite a decent Burgundy. It cost six shillings a bottle. Probably double that now. If you run short of money old Will Y. Darling will let you have some." (He spoke of a life-long friend of his, a Member of Parliament, an exceptional man who had successfully combined the drapery business with bookselling.)

I thought of my encounter with Sir Harold and the trouble that had caused. I promised myself that I would not invoke his aid or anyone else's. This time I was wrong. Sir William Darling was an altogether different sort of man to Sir Harold.

"I wish I was coming with you," he said, "but I've got this trouble you know." In his voice I detected a note of sadness. I thought of Mr. Wilkins. "I wish you were," I said. And I really meant it.

The Night Scot left King's Cross at ten fifteen. Mr.
Wilkins was so afraid that we should miss it that we
arrived at the station long before the train came in. I
had never seen him rattled before. Perhaps long years of
travelling with my father had reduced him to this state. Going
anywhere with my father by train was an even more nerve-
shattering experience than walking with him in the street.
Even when the train was actually in motion there was no way
of knowing whether he was on it or not. On the boat train
from Victoria he might appear just as it drew into Dover
Marine, remarking as he did so that he had had an interesting
"chat" with the Guard—on the other hand he might not.
He was not one of those people who always manage to catch
trains by the skin of their teeth, often he missed them altogether. The only way to deal with my father when travelling
with him was to provide oneself with a complete set of tickets
and documents and set off independently.

We made the journey from Great Marlborough Street to
King's Cross in three taxi cabs; Mr. Wilkins having noted
down the number of the taxi which was to proceed unescorted
in the little book he kept for his expenses. To me, accustomed
to Mediterranean taxis, it seemed an inadequate precaution.
With such a load, valued at, if not worth, several thousand
pounds, Alexandrian or Neapolitan taxi-men would have proceeded immediately to an outer suburb where our throats
would have been cut and the loot divided. But Mr. Wilkins
knew what he was doing. Here in London the drivers were
extremely reluctant to make the journey at all. Two of them
owned vehicles that were on the point of collapse; the other
man's was brand new and he was afraid of scratching it. Their
fears were justified. By the time we got to the station all three
were damaged.

We were seen off the premises by Brandon, the Porter. He

had stayed on late in order to lock up afterwards and set the burglar alarms. He was a little old man with a walrus moustache and an extremely independent mind, who had the interests of the business at heart. When not engaged in wrapping parcels and taking them to the post office in Wardour Street on a trolley he spent his time shoring-up the rapidly decaying fabric of the building. To this end he usually carried with him a long ladder.

"That's nice. I like that," he used to say to no one in particular, stopping to admire one of Miss Stallybrass's productions just as she was showing it to a customer "in the hand". "Nice bit of stuff!" and, picking up his ladder which he had put down in order to examine the garment more closely, went on his way humming something in a minor key that sounded like the Funeral March. Customers who were treated in this way were so taken aback that invariably they bought the model he had admired and, according to Miss Stallybrass, equally invariably sold it. As a result Brandon had the same kind of position in the hierarchy at Lane and Newby's as a chimney sweep at a fashionable wedding and if he failed to find anything worth stopping for whilst on passage through the showrooms it was regarded as a bad omen.

On this particular night he was a wild figure as he stood at the door of Number Fifty-Four dressed in a military greatcoat and a tweed motoring cap of my father's that was several sizes too large for him. In one hand he carried a truncheon at "the ready" which my father had insisted on issuing to him in case he was "set upon", in the other a candle lantern; around his neck on a cord he wore a police whistle. In spite of all this equipment he looked as though a gust of wind might blow him to smithereens.

"Well, if you're all right, I'll get locked up," he said as

soon as the six wicker baskets and the three cabin trunks had been squeezed aboard the three taxis, and without waiting for a reply slammed the front door in our faces with such violence that the ram's head knocker knocked itself—upon which Brandon's voice could be heard from inside asking, "Who's there?"

There was little to occupy us at King's Cross. Mr. Wilkins had talked me into arriving long before the time of departure on the grounds that there were certain formalities to be gone through with the luggage and that these might take some time. In fact the only formality was that of weighing it and this was speedily dispensed with when, at Mr. Wilkins' suggestion, I gave the man in charge of the machine a ten-shilling note. Now we stood shivering in the icy wind that howled down the platform. From time to time we were enveloped in clouds of acrid smoke; men with hammers passed, tapping the wheels of other trains, extracting from them a melancholy note. It was like a scene in *Anna Karenina*. I was angry with Mr. Wilkins. It seemed a bad beginning to our venture; but worse was to follow.

The Night Scot pulled in at last. The long line of sleeping cars with the attendants standing in the lighted doorways was redolent of warmth and comfort. I was looking forward to the journey. For years I had travelled in nothing more sumptuous than freight cars and cattle trucks. The last time I had travelled on the Night Scot was in 1940. I had pleasant memories of it: the clean drugget on the floor; the bed-clothes turned down neatly; the spare blanket; the multiplicity of reading lights and ventilators; the little velvet cushion to save one's pocket watch from shock; the train itself thundering through the Borders in the first faint light of the morning; the hot tea and biscuits brought by the attendant half an hour before it got in to Waverley.

As the train came to a standstill I asked Mr. Wilkins which coach we were to occupy.

"It's at the far end," he said.

At the very end there was a single coach of ordinary, non-sleeping compartments, First Class and Third. The porter took our luggage, Mr. Wilkins' diminutive suit-case that was like a sardine tin with a handle and my own bulging zip bag, and made for a Third-Class Smoker. He placed Mr. Wilkins' case on the rack above a window seat with its back to the engine and my own at the opposite end of the compartment next to the corridor facing the engine. All the seats were reserved.

Mr. Wilkins had prudently vanished. He was supervising the loading of the heavy baggage. By the time he returned the compartment was beginning to fill up. I noticed that everyone was carrying rugs and wearing heavy overcoats. I had brought a raincoat. My father had advised me to do so. "You don't want to clutter yourself up with a greatcoat at your age," he said.

"I thought you'd booked sleepers?" I said to Mr. Wilkins. Mr. Wilkins said nothing.

"Do you realise that we shall be sitting in this compartment for more than eight hours? It'll be absolute hell."

Mr. Wilkins still said nothing. He gave me a basilisk stare.

"You might at least have got me a window seat. This is the worst place in the whole damn compartment." By now I was really angry. Our companions were beginning to take an interest in what I was saying. I was forced to lower my voice. "What the hell's the idea?" I hissed.

"Saving expenses," said Mr. Wilkins.

I set off down the train to find a sleeper. The whole of the first car was reserved for the Ministry of Fuel and Power.

Although the train was due to leave in a few minutes it was still entirely empty.

"They're joining at Grantham," said the attendant. "And there's a waiting list as long as your arm. There's been a war you know." He was not as helpful as the attendant I remembered on my last trip in the Night Scot.

According to the lists that were posted up at the door of each coach, the rest of the train seemed to be occupied by Lieutenant-Commanders Royal Navy, Members of Parliament and members of the Wholesale, natty little men in herring-bone overcoats and silk shirts who were now beginning to arrive, trotting up the platform dwarfed by model girls in next seasons' coats who towered above them. Whatever these manufacturers were going to show would certainly not be "in the hand".

The First-Class compartments in the other half of our carriage were less crowded. Most of them had only three occupants, but they were already engaged in constructing make-shift couches for the night. To join them would simply create the conditions which already existed in our own compartment.

The journey was a nightmare. Of the five people in the compartment two were drunk, the others were very merry. The drunks argued acrimoniously in undertones. At intervals they refreshed themselves with British wine. The three merry ones were Poles, who played an interminable and noisy variant of Snap on an upturned suit-case.

As soon as the train left King's Cross Mr. Wilkins prepared himself for bed. He took off his bowler hat, removed his teeth and his front collar stud, both of which he placed in his waistcoat pocket, loosened his bootlaces and fell instantly into a deep sleep.

Except for Mr. Wilkins and myself the other occupants of the compartment were in a state of ferment throughout the night. Between them they formed an almost constant proces-

sion to the lavatory. As, one by one, they went out, leaving
the door open, they trod heavily on my feet. To begin with I
shut it, but no sooner had I done so than they returned and
the whole process was repeated in reverse.

The train stopped twice during the night—at Grantham
and at Newcastle. At intervals a collector arrived to clip the
tickets. As Mr. Wilkins had somehow contrived to give me
his ticket as well as my own he was able to sleep undisturbed.
The two men who had drunk too much had also omitted to
purchase tickets and as they had no money there was a great
deal of taking of names and addresses. (They were in fact in
the wrong train, having intended to travel to Manchester
from Euston.) The one who was my neighbour and who spent
the night lying partly on top of me, endeavoured to borrow
the fare.

After Grantham, the compartment, which up to then had
been stifling hot, became very cold. The smoke from innumerable cigarettes hung in the gelid air. There was no way of
extinguishing the lights even if one had dared to do so. I had
nothing to read except the *Evening Standard* and I had read
it whilst waiting for the train at King's Cross.

For all its proud name the Night Scot was an hour late at
Edinburgh. With some difficulty I woke Mr. Wilkins. At first
I thought that he was dead. His mouth was wide open in a
ghastly grin which I associated with rigor-mortis; but suddenly he came-to, put his teeth back, adjusted his collar stud
and replaced his bowler hat.

"I trust that you slept well, Mr. Eric," he said, shamelessly.
"We've got a heavy day in front of us."

CHAPTER SIXTEEN

CALEDONIA STERN AND WILD

A PORTER from the hotel was on the platform to meet us. "You're in Number Five, Mr. Willukins. Your usual," he said, touching his cap. "I'll look after the skips."

The way to the Station Hotel led through a maze of grubby passages, flanked by large chocolate-coloured photographs of Scottish scenery, all of which looked as if they had been exposed in a steady drizzle. Soon we found ourselves in a part of the hotel not normally seen by the public where we met scullions from the kitchens on errands with covered buckets.

We were welcomed by a senior porter with an air of authority and shiny, quick eyes, like a bird's.

"You're in Number Five, Mr. Willukins," he said—and to me. "How is Mr. Newby—I haven't seen him since the war —and Mrs. Newby? I remember they used to have a big sitting-room upstairs. Times change. He was a fine man, Mr. Newby." He made it sound like a dirge.

In spite of the warmth of the welcome it was difficult to be enraptured by the room to which we were now escorted.

Stockroom Number Five was a tall, narrow room illuminated by a fifty-watt bulb. The decorations had once been beige but the efforts to clean them had resulted in the walls becoming one great smear. The only furniture was a number of cane chairs and two trestle tables which were covered with white sheets that had been neatly patched. The effect was of a mortuary or a place where members of the Reformed Church might pray together before proceeding to England by train.

In addition to these rudimentary furnishings there was a telephone that had once been black and which was now the colour of old bones, and a dog-eared telephone book on which a succession of commercial travellers, made desperate by the inadequacies of the telephone system, had doodled frenziedly as they waited for calls to Kilmarnock and Galashiels that never came through. The view from the window, which was surprisingly clean, took in the roof of the Waverley Station and one span of the North Bridge. At intervals the entire prospect was blotted out by clouds of smoke.

"I thought we were having a sitting-room," I said. I felt too wretched to show any spirit.

"All the sitting-rooms were booked," said Mr. Wilkins. "Besides . . ."

"It saves expense!"

"Let's have breakfast," said Mr. Wilkins.

"What about a bath and shave?"

"Time's getting on." He took a gold watch from his pocket. "Half past eight. Our first appointment's at nine-thirty and we have to unpack."

In spite of not having shaved his face was as smooth as butter. Mine resembled a gooseberry.

Breakfast was like a slow-motion film of a ritual. At intervals rather smelly waitresses brought food, but with none of the supporting things that makes breakfast possible. Butter arrived without toast; porridge without milk; tea without sugar. In obedience to some defunct regulation there was only one bowl of sugar to four tables, every few minutes it disappeared completely.* Other commercials seemed better

* The Station Hotel is a vastly different place today.

served—they munched lugubriously, immersed in their *Expresses* and *Daily Mails*—a few like ourselves gazed in the direction of the kitchens or half-rose in their seats in an extremity of despair.

By the time we had finished breakfast it was ten past nine. In twenty minutes the first customer was due to arrive.

There was no time to wash or shave. We raced to the Stockroom. To me it seemed inconceivable that one night in a cabin trunk could have wreaked such havoc upon dresses that had been packed with such care. Mrs. Ribble's crêpes looked as though they had been used for the purpose of garrotting someone. Even the woollen dresses looked as though they had been trampled underfoot as I hung them on the rails which had been provided by the stockroom porter. Only Mr. Wilkins' coats and suits, heavy, tailored garments, had escaped unscathed. By this time I was used to Mr. Wilkins' monopoly of good fortune. He seemed to bear a charmed life.

" Now, Mr. Eric," said Mr. Wilkins, " this is the programme for today."

It was now nine-twenty-seven. He handed me a sheet of hotel writing paper, part of a large supply which he had filched on the way to breakfast, on which he had drawn up a time-table:

```
9-30  Mrs. McHaggart, Robertsons, Edinburgh
10-30 Mrs. McHavers, Lookies, Dundee
11-00 Miss McTush, Campbells, Edinburgh
11-45 Mrs. McRobbie, Alexander McGregor, Edinburgh
2-30  Miss Wilkie, McNoons of Perth
4-30  Miss Reekie, Madame Vera, Edinburgh
```

To me it seemed more like a gathering of the clans in some

rainswept glen than an assignation to buy dresses in the sub-
basement of a Railway Hotel.

In the three minutes that remained to us before the arrival
of Mrs. McHaggart, Mr. Wilkins briefed me on their idio-
syncrasies. Just as a last-minute revision outside the examina-
tion hall is useless so Mr. Wilkins' brilliant summing-up only
increased my confusion.

"Mrs. McHaggart is a good Buyer but she doesn't like us
to serve any of the other stores in Princes Street. Of course we
do—it wouldn't be worth coming here otherwise—and she
knows it. The women here know everything," he said,
gloomily. "You can't keep anything from them. They all
have friends and relatives in one another's shops.

"What we have to do is to get Mrs. McHaggart's order
down on paper. If it's good enough then we don't show the
things she's chosen to Miss McTush. They're enemies. If we
get a poor order from Mrs. McHaggart then we show everything to Miss McTush and change the styles. Miss McTush
knows we do this so we can't change them very much.
Mrs. McRobbie is the same as Mrs. McHaggart and Miss
McTush. She's in Princes Street too. The important thing
is to keep the three of them from meeting. If they do
at least one of them won't give us an order; that's why
I've put in Mrs. McHavers between Mrs. McHaggart and
Miss McTush, because she comes from Dundee. Miss
McTush doesn't really mind what Mrs. McHaggart and
Mrs. McRobbie buy as long as she gets her delivery before they do. In fact we deliver to them all at the same
time—we don't dare do otherwise—so Miss McTush is just
as difficult as the others. Mrs. McHaggart only buys Coats
and Suits and two-pieces. She's not supposed to buy two-
pieces but she does. That's why we don't see Miss Cameron,
the Dress Buyer. Miss McTush buys everything. Mrs. Mc-

Robbie buys everything. Miss Reekie can buy anything but usually she buys nothing. She's a most difficult woman. I call her 'The Old Stinker'," said Mr. Wilkins, "on account of her name being Reekie. I usually take Miss McTush and Mrs. McHavers out to lunch together because Mrs. McHavers comes from Dundee. On Tuesday I take Mrs. McHaggart. First thing on Tuesday morning I call on the ones who haven't given us an appointment. With luck we see some of them in the afternoon or on Wednesday morning. We usually manage to get off to Glasgow on Wednesday afternoon for an appointment in the evening."

"Don't you give Mrs. McRobbie lunch?"

"She's got an ulcer. She never eats lunch. I like Mrs. McRobbie," said Mr. Wilkins.

"What about the evenings?"

"If you want to take Buyers out in the evening, Mr. Eric, that's your affair," said Mr. Wilkins. "Personally I drink beer."

As he said this there was a murmuring sound outside the door and Mrs. McHaggart appeared. We were off.

Mrs. McHaggart was tall and thin. She wore an air of preternatural gloom that was accentuated by a small drip on the end of her nose. In all the years that I was to know Mrs. McHaggart the drop never actually dripped but always remained suspended. She was dressed in claret-coloured tweed and a fur of a kind that was unknown to me, made perhaps from the skins of animals trapped north of the Highland Line, over which hung an aura compounded of moth-balls and Parma Violets. She asked after my parents in a kind way, but her manner of doing so suggested that they were either dead or on the point of dying. In this way she resembled the Stockroom Porter.

To give Mr. Wilkins full play for his undoubted powers in

dealing with a customer such as Mrs. McHaggart I ordered coffee and biscuits from room-service on the telephone—itself no mean feat—whilst she enumerated a list of her acquaintances who were also on the point of dissolution.

"Well, Mr. Willukins, I suppose I'm the first," said Mrs. McHaggart with a faint air of menace, as she nibbled a biscuit and sipped her coffee.

"As always, the first, Mrs. McHaggart," said Mr. Wilkins, rising gallantly to the bait. "*Nulli Secundus*. Second to None."

"I expect you have a very full day," said Mrs. McHaggart remorselessly. "You have so many customers, have you not, Mr. Willukins?"

"We have a good number of customers, Mrs. McHaggart."

"All in Edinburgh, I suppose?"

"I am happy to say that we have a large country connection, Mrs. McHaggart," said Mr. Wilkins, evading her, I thought, superbly. "In fact I think you know Mrs. McHavers of Lookies of Dundee. She will be arriving quite soon." He fished out his massive gold hunter and looked at it with an air of pantomime. "To be precise at half past ten—in twenty-minutes time."

"Then you'll be in no hurry for me," said Mrs. McHaggart. "I don't want to be in her way. There's a special customer of mine coming into the shop at half past ten. I think I'll slip back and see to her. I can come back here later. If you're busy, Mr. Willukins, Mr. Newby will look after me. Will you not, Mr. Newby? About eleven-thirty." Triumphantly she rose to go.

I was gibbering with apprehension. If Mrs. McHaggart returned at eleven-thirty the disastrous conjunction with Miss McTush might occur. She would certainly meet Mrs. McRobbie at eleven forty-five.

It was Mr. Wilkins who saved the situation, at least temporarily.

"Mrs. McHaggart," he said. "I think that it is only fair to tell you that this is the first time that Mr. Eric has shown a collection. I think he might find it a little difficult, that is why I suggest that you make your selection now. Perhaps you will allow me to show you some of our productions."

Without explaining why it would be difficult for me he unhooked a coat from the rail and cast it before her with an air that was both gallant and at the same time obsequious. The coat was powder blue with a fox collar—one of our more " dressy " productions. I only hoped the floor was clean. At this moment Mr. Wilkins seemed to me a curious mixture of Sir Walter Raleigh and Uriah Heep.

"Lovely, isn't it? " he said.

Mrs. McHaggart was baulked. "Very well," she said. First round to Mr. Wilkins.

I helped Mr. Wilkins with his coats by opening the pattern book for Mrs. McHaggart, but all the time I was thinking of my dresses. What would happen if nobody bought them? What sort of woman was Mrs. McHavers? It was true that my father had spent a lot of time telling me about her, but now I was so confused that I was no longer capable of telling a McHavers from a McTush.

Mrs. McHavers was a few minutes late for her appointment. This was unfortunate as it gave Mrs. McHaggart the excuse to reduce her rate of striking. It was obvious that she was as intent on discovering the identity of the customer who was arriving at eleven o'clock as we were on preventing her.

Mrs. McHavers turned out to be large and fat and happy. She wore a remarkable hat, a red velvet bonnet with a cairngorm embedded in it, a stone so enormous that it would have been more at home on the landing of a geological museum than stuck in a hat. She didn't care about the McTushes, the McHaggarts or the McRobbies. It was easy for her to be broad-minded in Dundee. If she too had been from Edinburgh she would have been just like the rest.

"How's business at Robertson's? " she shouted across the room to Mrs. McHaggart in a voice that made her wince. "Everyone tells me that you've been having a difficult time."

It was obvious that Mrs. McHaggart did not take this at all well.

"That's the trouble with Edinburgh," Mrs. McHavers said in a loud aside. "They all live on investments. Afraid to get their hands dirty. Now in Dundee we're not doing too badly in spite of Jute being in a terrible way." And then: "Well, let's get on with it, Mr. Newby. No good moaning over the dead."

I showed her my little collection. "Bit different, isn't it? " she said. "Different handwriting. Well, what are you waiting for, Mr. Newby? Don't you want an order? "

I was so nervous that I could hardly write. Worse still I had forgotten the code in which the prices were written on the tickets.

"Here, let me do it," said Mrs. McHavers, seizing the order book.

In fifteen minutes the whole order was written down. I had had to improvise the prices as we went along. On some dresses I had grossly overcharged; on others the result was a greatly reduced margin of profit. Overall the result was about right. It was a good order.

"I'll be back at the hotel at twelve-thirty," she said as I escorted her to the lift. "Don't worry about me, I'll find my own way out. You'd better get back to the Stockroom and get rid of Mrs. McHaggart, otherwise there'll be trouble."

It was now five minutes to eleven. In the Stockroom Mr.

Wilkins was still writing down Mrs. McHaggart's order. There were still four coats to go.

At any moment Miss McTush might appear.

At two minutes to eleven Mr. Wilkins' head appeared, dramatically, in a gap in the rail of coats.

"Main Hall! Miss McTush. Head her off!" he said in a stage whisper.

Two lifts operated between the Stockroom floor and the Main Hall. There was no public staircase. If Miss McTush had already begun her descent then we would pass one another like ships at night time in a narrow channel. On the other hand it was too dangerous to wait for her below. At any moment Mrs. McHaggart might emerge from the Stockroom.

There was an interminable wait for the lift. The liftman seemed to have died on one of the upper floors. When it finally arrived I was conveyed straightway to the third floor where a reception was in progress. As a result I arrived too late in the Main Hall.

"There she goes," said the Head Porter in the cheerful voice which human beings reserve for one another's misfortunes. I had a momentary glimpse of a sturdy, fur-coated figure entering the lift which I had just got out of.

"I must get to the Stockroom before she does," I said. "It's a matter of life or death."

He was not the Head Porter of the North British Hotel for nothing. The door of the lift was already shut. Before I could say another word he had crossed the hall and was pressing one of the buttons.

"You've got two minutes," he said. "Go through that door and follow the staircase down through the kitchens. You're old Mr. Newby's son, aren't you? He was always up to this kind of caper."

I descended the stairs three steps at a time. It was like going down into the bowels of a battleship. At the moment when Miss McTush emerged from the lift in all her panoply I, too, arrived in the corridor.

"Miss McTush? " I said. "My name's Newby."

She started to tell me about the lift.

"I wonder if you would mind coming upstairs for a few minutes," I said. "Mrs. Mc . . . Mr. Wilkins has a customer who is taking rather a long time to put her order down. She's just finishing. We could have some coffee in the lounge."

"I've had my coffee," said Miss McTush.

"Would you care for a drink? "

"I never drink when I'm working," said Miss McTush. She was regarding me with a humorous eye. "But I know when I'm not wanted. We'll sit in the lounge until Mr. Wilkins has finished with Mrs. McHaggart."

In a few minutes Mr. Wilkins appeared.

"I'm sorry we had to delay you, Miss McTush," he said, bending over her hand. "I had a country customer who took a long time to put down her order."

While Miss McTush was being shown the collection there was a knock at the door. Fortunately Mr. Wilkins had bolted it. It was Mrs. McHaggart. "I think I left my gloves here," she said, trying to dart past me into the Stockroom.

"Here they are, Mr. Newby," said Mr. Wilkins. I had never seen him move so fast. "Nice to see you again, Mrs. McHaggart," beaming over my shoulder. "I am looking forward to our luncheon immensely."

It had been arranged that Mr. Wilkins should take Mrs. McHaggart to lunch whilst I should deal with Miss McTush and Mrs. McHavers. Mr. Wilkins was to have the North British Hotel while I was to use the George Hotel, which was half a mile away. It was impossible to include Mrs. McRobbie in these complex arrangements. She was to be regarded as a separate problem and given lunch on Tuesday. As it happened she failed to turn up for her appointment. It seemed a fool-proof arrangement, but we had reckoned without the devilish ingenuity of Mrs. McHaggart. At twelve-forty-five I set off with Mrs. McHavers and Miss McTush for the George Hotel. In the ten minutes which they allowed themselves to powder their noses I managed to shave and change my shirt. Although I was now more or less presentable, emotionally I was exhausted. The childish evasions of the morning, following upon a night without sleep, had left me in a light-headed condition. At the hotel we went straight to the table. My guests, unburdened of the cares of buying, made themselves agreeable. They drank gin and tonics. To my relief they both ordered a nourishing meal without succumbing to the temptation of choosing those items on the menu which are listed according to their availability without any mention of price. I relaxed. Soon I found that, just like my father, I too was telling little jokes. The waiters began to look apprehensively at our table.

We were eating our shrimp and lobster cocktails when, to my horror I saw Mrs. McHaggart enter the restaurant. Stumping up behind her was Mr. Wilkins. She made straight for our table. I rose to my feet with my mouth full of sea-food.

"Ah, Mr. Newby," she said, ignoring my guests. "This is a surprise. Mr. Willukins, you should have told me that Mr. Newby was having a party. I wouldn't have come."

Mr. Wilkins said nothing. He had the air of a man on the way to the scaffold who has been halted in order to be given a stirrup cup.

"Won't you join us?" I said. "I'm sure that Mrs. McHavers and Miss McTush will be delighted."

"If you insist," said Mrs. McHaggart. "I think it would be very nice. Don't you, Mr. Willukins?"

"Rather heavy going, Mr. Eric," said Mr. Wilkins as we stood outside the hotel watching three separate Rolls-Royce taxis as they carried our guests about their lawful occasions.

"Not really a success."

"Disastrous."

"Why did you bring Mrs. McHaggart to the George when you said you were going to give her lunch at the North British?"

"We were just going into the restaurant when she noticed a manufacturer with whom she was not on good terms whom she wished to avoid. The next thing we were in a taxi on the way here. I don't think she saw anyone at all. I think she made him up."

"Do you think she'll cancel the order?"

"I don't know," said Mr. Wilkins. "In all the years I've been coming to Edinburgh I've never known anything like this before. Your father and I had some narrow shaves but nothing like this."

He managed to make it sound as though the whole thing was directly attributable to me. "We'd better get back to the N.B.," he said. "We've got Miss Wilkie of McNoons of Perth in ten minutes."

At the hotel there was a message awaiting us from Miss Wilkie. A mourning order of unparalleled proportions was engaging her attention in Perth. Would Thursday do?

"She must think that we live here," said Mr. Wilkins. "But all the same I'd like to get my teeth into that mourning order." It was an unseemly metaphor.

He spent the next hour in telephoning to remote parts of Scotland in an endeavour to inveigle Buyers to visit us. The formula was invariable. According to Mr. Wilkins putting through personal calls to Buyers were useless. After costly delays the Buyer would be brought to the telephone. Thereafter the conversation was punctuated at three-minute intervals by costly peeps.

"Hallo," he said, "Wilkins here of Lane and Newby of London. Good afternoon, Miss Pettigrew . . . Delightful to hear your voice. PEEP, PEEP, PEEP . . . I'm speaking from the North British Hotel, Edinburgh . . . I trust that you are in good health . . . Oh, I'm sorry to hear that . . . Most unfortunate . . . It must be very painful . . . You've been working too hard. PEEP, PEEP, PEEP . . . Yes, all well . . . Marvellous for his age . . . Miss Pettigrew, I thought perhaps you might like to run over here tomorrow. (The vision of Miss Pettigrew setting off from Stirling in a blizzard dressed in running shorts was irresistible.) "We're showing some very nice coats and costumes——"

"And dresses," I hissed. "Tell her about the dresses."

"And dresses," said Mr. Wilkins, obediently, but with less enthusiasm, . . . "Yes, I know you thought they were expensive, but that was some years ago. I think that it was in 1938 that I last had the pleasure of serving you . . . PEEP, PEEP, PEEP . . . Of course, the handwriting's changed. Young Mr. Newby's with us now. He's gingering us up." Mr. Wilkins laughed, rather unpleasantly, I thought . . . "I'll contact you the next time we're in Edinburgh . . . Perhaps you might like us to bring a few things to Stirling . . . Good-bye, Miss Pettigrew . . . PEEP, PEEP, PEEP . . . Delightful to hear from you."

After the awful night to which Mr. Wilkins had condemned me I was in no mood to be merciful. "Tell me," I said as he ran his pencil through the last of these forlorn hopes. "Have we ever done any business at all with these people you've been telephoning? It seems a waste of money to me."

"Mr. Eric, in this business one must never neglect an

opportunity. One must keep in touch," he said, with a complete lack of conviction.

"But what's the good of keeping in touch with people who don't want to be kept in touch with?"

"Huh, Huh, Huh!" said Mr. Wilkins. "You're just like your father, Mr. Eric. He always enjoyed a joke when he was on the journey."

Miss Reekie proved to be every bit as awful as Mr. Wilkins had said she would be. We spent four hours showing her the collection. "Showing" was a misnomer. She worked over it like a rag-picker on a rubbish dump. At the end of this time, filled to the brim with tea, boiled eggs and whisky she had whittled down the collection, some hundred items, to three coats, two suits and one dress. Even then she was undecided.

"You boys must be tired of me," she said. "I know I'm a difficult old faggot."

"Not at all, Miss Reekie," said Mr. Wilkins, managing a ghastly grin. "At Lane and Newby's we also serve who only stand and wait."

It was better than I could have managed after four hours with Miss Reekie. All I wanted her to do was to go away. In the end she bought nothing but offered to come back the next day. There were no takers. She came all the same.

"I think we deserve a drink, Mr. Eric," said Mr. Wilkins when Miss Reekie had departed. "I'll treat you to the finest glass of beer in Scotland.'

I thought so too. I had a raging thirst. The only way in which we had been able to show our disapproval of her had been by total abstention. Now I was too far gone to quibble over the word treat as used by Mr. Wilkins. Without a word I followed him.

In the downstairs bar of the North British Hotel, a place which no longer exists, we drank William Younger's Heavy

Gravity in company with other commercials recovering from an awful day. After what I had been through in the last twenty-four hours it seemed like heaven. Women were not admitted. No one spoke except to order more. The Barmaid was an elderly lady who was a fanatic about her beer although she had never tasted it.

"Ay, it's guid beer, real guid beer and for why?" she demanded, resting her arms on the bar. "Because I keep the pipes clean. Clean pipes, that's the secret."

After four pints of Heavy Gravity neither Mr. Wilkins nor I cared whether the pipes were clean or not and after sharing a packet of cachew nuts we decided to go to bed.

For some impenetrable reason Mr. Wilkins had booked a double room. It could not have been for the reasons of economy because the price was exactly double that of a single one.

The chambermaid had laid out my pyjamas and dressing-gown on the bed and hung my spare suit on one of the cupboards. Only Mr. Wilkins' minute suitcase which was locked had resisted her efforts.

I was longing to see what he carried inside it. I did not have to wait long. With surprising swiftness he took off his boots and hung his suit over a chair. He then removed his shirt, revealing a complete suit of thick, long, woollen underwear. Opening his suitcase he removed from it his shaving things, a toothbrush and a pair of flannel pyjamas which he proceeded to put on over his underclothes. Inside the suitcase there remained nothing but a spare stiff collar. The journey was due to last ten days. I was more impressed than I dared to say.

"Would you like to bath first?" I said. "I'm in no hurry."

But I was too late. Mr. Wilkins had already removed his teeth. His reply was incomprehensible. Even as he spoke he fell asleep and although I got up several times and turned him over all through the night he snored stertorously like a man in apoplexy.

The following day was no less exacting. I spent most of the morning trying to interest Miss Cameron of Robertsons in my productions. She was the one who had been Mrs. McHaggart's best friend until Mrs. McHaggart had pirated her dresses and jackets. It was useless, the iron had entered her soul. In the afternoon Miss Reekie came back and ordered a dress and Mrs. McHaggart and Miss McTush sent their assistants to cut down their orders.

On Wednesday afternoon we left for Glasgow. At Edinburgh Mr. Wilkins had taken orders for several thousand pounds. Mine totalled nine hundred. Most of the orders were for Mrs. Ribble's crêpe dinner dresses.

"Not too bad for the first time, Mr. Eric," said Mr. Wilkins. "At least you've covered your expenses." He was seated opposite me in a Third-Class Smoker. All pretence at luxury had been abandoned.

This was cold comfort to me. Besides I did not understand what Mr. Wilkins meant when he spoke of "covering my expenses". So far I had paid for everything: taxis, the lunch at the George, two lugubrious evenings of beer drinking and the tremendous bill at the North British which included Miss Reekie's potations—I had also done all the tipping. My money was evaporating at an alarming rate. I was not only covering my own expenses but Mr. Wilkins as well. I resolved to speak to him about it.

I was about to do so when the train entered a tunnel and speech became impossible. When it emerged the view from the window was so apocalyptical that I forgot all about it. I looked out on a waste land filled with stagnant pools and the remains of bicycles. From the top of a muddy hillock a band of urchins were about to launch a pram on a muddy version of the Cresta Run. As the train went past the pram began to move downhill. In it there was a large placid-looking baby, sitting bolt upright. It seemed quite unimpressed. On the hill behind there was a large Victorian Cemetery.

Another minute and we arrived in Glasgow.

The hotel in Glasgow seemed less forbidding than the North British in Edinburgh. The terrible smells of kitchen were less pronounced. We also had a sitting-room on one of the upper floors, one which Lane and Newby had occupied regularly for more than forty years. Even Mr. Wilkins could not very well demur as there were no stockrooms. To my relief I managed to get a single room—after a night on a train with Mr. Wilkins and two more listening to him snoring in Edinburgh I was exhausted.

At six o'clock we had an appointment with the Misses McAndrew. They were sisters who came from a town on the Borders where they had built up a remarkable business among the upper classes. McAndrew's was one of the few accounts from which it was possible to get a better order for dresses than for coats and it had been drummed into me by everyone concerned that failure to do so was tantamount to disaster. "That's just the thing for McAndrew's!" my mother used to say when some particularly simple dress appeared from the model workroom and she would send them a sketch of it together with some patterns. Sometimes she used to get an order but more often a letter would arrive which indicated in no uncertain terms that the dress did not come up to the McAndrew standard.

"We are *most disappointed* with the sketch you have sent us of the wool dress 'Gun Club' wrote one or other of the Misses McAndrew (it was impossible to tell which from the letter as their literary style was identical). "It seems to us that you are not *au fait* with the requirements of our ladies. They do not want *mass-produced* garments. Please *do not* send us any further sketches or patterns unless you are convinced that they are really suitable. At the moment you are involving us in considerable *postal expenditure* and all to no purpose."

The Misses McAndrew were unlike any other Buyers I had ever seen. They gave the impression that they had never stooped to anything as low as commerce. They were very quiet ladies with silver hair, beautifully dressed in rare tweeds and minimal quantities of excellent fur. They arrived on the first stroke of six and without delay settled down to work.

After ten minutes it was obvious that things were not going well. As I showed dress after dress with the Misses McAndrew looking grimly at them the quietness which I had first remarked in them as a lady-like quality now seemed to assume a more sinister significance.

"No, Mr. Newby!"

"Not that, Mr. Newby!"

"Our ladies would not wear such a garment, Mr. Newby!"

"No, Mr. Newby!"

"That is not at all the kind of thing we require, Mr. Newby!"

Sometimes they said nothing at all but simply looked in eloquent silence.

I felt my nerve going. I was in the presence of twin intelligences of a sort that I had never before encountered. Intelligence that was linked with a highly developed and individual sense of style. Even now when I was showing them all the wrong things, I knew what they wanted—the difficulty was to provide it.

"Now this," I said, holding up the last dress in the collection that I dared to show them, a wool georgette in a washed out shade of green that everyone else had bought, "is the sort of thing . . ."

"No, Mr. Newby!"

Together they rose to their feet adjusting their pieces of sable.

"Lovely, aren't they?" said Mr. Wilkins, choosing this inopportune moment to come forward and put his foot in it.

Both sisters gave him a withering look.

"Mr. Willukins," said the younger of the two who looked even more deceptively gentle than the other, "How often do we have to tell you that our customers are not the sort who wear wool georgette." She made it sound as though some stigma might result from contact with the stuff.

"For the most part they spend their time in outdoor pursuits. They need fine checks for indoors and really thick tweeds for the hills."

There was not a moment to lose. It was obvious that she was pronouncing a funeral oration over my collection. I picked up one of Mr. Wilkins' swatches of suit patterns. They were fine saxonies intended for men's suits and because of this they were three times as expensive as the materials I would normally have used for such a purpose.

"That's what we want, Mr. Newby," one of them said, instantly. "Now all we need are three simple styles in which they can be made."

I took the three simplest styles in the collection and said that they would be even more simple. I managed to convince them that what they would get would be little more than tubes of material with four holes in them. I also said that they would be very expensive, which was true.

"To our customers," the elder Miss McAndrew said. "Expense is a secondary consideration. The important thing, Mr. Newby, is satisfaction. Satisfaction and quality."

"We could also have the dresses made with jackets. Like that," she indicated one of Mr. Wilkins' suits, 'but no padding in the shoulders."

"And horn buttons," said her sister.

"Horn buttons and leather belts for the dresses. The belts must be of the finest quality. We want none of your *Wholesale Belts*."

"Two-pieces," said Mr. Wilkins, waking up suddenly. "I do the two-pieces."

'They are too dressed-up for our ladies, Mr. Wilkins," one of them said firmly. "They require them for shooting."

For a moment I had an insane desire to ask what.

"This is the kind of material we need," she went on, looking through a swatch of twenty-one-ounce tweeds intended for gamekeepers. "For our ladies to wear on the hills. With horn buttons. Providing that they do not cost more than thirty guineas you can write the order. You can confirm the price to us later. And remember—no padding in the shoulders."

It was the biggest order I had had. They ordered the saxony dresses in three different styles and six different colours. They also ordered the two-pieces in a number of permutations of colour and style. I calculated that two thicknesses of the twenty-ounce tweed would be almost bullet-proof. Perhaps that was what the Misses McAndrew intended.

Made amicable by having found what they wanted they then proceeded to order a surprisingly large number of black chiffon dinner dresses.

One of these dresses was so expensive that so far I had only succeeded in selling one to Miss Reekie and then only by agreeing to let her have the model at a reduced price. In fact

I had already decided to withdraw it from the collection. Although extremely elegant its effect seemed to be too sepulchral for the wholesale.

It was an extraordinary order—the combination of the heavy tweeds and the funereally graceful chiffons. When not engaged in killing things the McAndrew's customers seemed to spend their evening dining in a family vault.

When the McAndrews had gone Mr. Wilkins tried to persuade me that this order would more properly be executed by his department, but the memory of the railway journey, the double room, the expenses, was fresh in my mind and I hardened my heart. It was already pretty hard.

I countered by asking him about the expenses.

"I'm getting very short of money. Either you'll have to give me some or else you'll have to pay from now on; at least until we leave Glasgow."

"I haven't got any to spare," he said.

"But you haven't spent anything yet."

"There are certain expenses," he said, mysteriously. "Besides, we have to keep separate accounts. I suggest that you send for some more."

Arguing with Mr. Wilkins I found difficulty in deciding whether I was dealing with a diabolical intelligence or with an idiot.

"I know we have to keep separate accounts but the money all comes from the same source and we've been given it for the same purpose. It doesn't belong to us."

"I like to keep it separate," said Mr. Wilkins.

"Well, what do you think I've been doing up to now. I've been paying for everything."

"I thought you wanted to pay. After all, Mr. Eric, it's all the same in the end whoever puts it down."

By now I was furious.

"Why don't you want to put down your expenses?" I shouted. "Dammit, tell me!"

I made so much noise that there was a hammering on the wall and a voice said "Quiet!"

Mr. Wilkins said nothing. His face was shiny.

The thought of Miss Gatling waiting to pounce on me when I returned to Great Marlborough Street made me desperate.

"Mr. Wilkins," I said. "If you don't put up the money for our expenses I shall telephone Miss Gatling and tell her that you refuse to pay your share."

For the second time in my acquaintance with Mr. Wilkins a trace of emotion showed itself on the smooth expanse of his face. It was impossible to say what the emotion was but it twitched.

"Will five pounds be any help?" he said.

"No!" I handed him a sheet of paper on which I had written down our joint expenses.

"I don't think all these expenses were necessary," he said after looking at it intently for some time. "Besides, I thought you were treating me to the beer."

"It was you who asked me in the first place. You can perfectly well put it down as 'dinner'. If you choose to drink your dinner instead of eating it nobody's going to question that."

In the end after much grumbling Mr. Wilkins paid his share; but afterwards he always insisted on each of us paying for our own drinks. This proved a great nuisance. The waiters got in a fearful mess with the change and because neither I nor Mr. Wilkins were prepared to tip for one another they often failed to get anything at all.

For the rest of the week we did rather badly in Glasgow. Originally we had planned to leave on Saturday morning but as a result of one of Mr. Wilkins' more than usually ill-timed telephone calls a customer from Ayr decided to visit us on Saturday afternoon. She never appeared and as a result we found ourselves marooned in Glasgow for the week-end.

All Saturday and all Sunday it rained in torrents. In such weather, equipped with nothing but a business suit it was impossible to go into the country. On Saturday evening we went to the pictures. On Sunday morning, returning to my room after a late breakfast, I met the occupant of the next sitting-room, the man who had shouted "Quiet" when we had been quarrelling over our expenses. He was one of the manufacturers whom I had first seen on the platform at King's Cross. Since then I had seen him often. Each time one of our customers arrived at our door or was on the point of leaving he too opened his door to see what he was missing.

Now he was standing outside on the landing smoking a cigar. On the door of his sitting-room was a crudely lettered placard.

Sweetie-Pie Models (1946) Ltd.
Wholesale Couture and Export
Director. Harry Goldfinch
Great Portland Street.

Until this moment Mr. Goldfinch had only glared at me. Now he adopted a more ingratiating approach. For him too, the Sabbath was a day of rest. Perhaps, like me, he was lonely and far from home.

"My name's Goldfinch," he said, superfluously. "Everyone calls me Harry." We shook hands.

"What a terrible place and a terrible weather. And I have to stay in this dump. And do you know why? Because my customer stood me up. She came here Friday. Saw the stuff. Had some drinks. Dinner at the Central. Nice big dinner.

Then she was going to come back here and put her order down. Came back from powdering her nose to say she'd have to come in Monday morning or she'd miss her train. Train to where? You know what that was? An excuse to spend the week-end with her boy friend in Glasgow. You know what he is? An agent! Here in Glasgow, Tink-a-Bell Gowns. What can you do with a woman like that, I ask you? " Mr. Gold-finch opened his arms in a gesture of despair. " Any rate here I am. I don't know what Mrs. Goldfinch will say when I get back," he went on. " She made a terrible fuss on the telephone when I told her I wouldn't be back—mostly on account of the girl.

" You see I've got a model girl," he said, confidentially. " You must have one for a high-class business like this. The money I've spent on that girl! Couldn't spell her own name when I took her on. Now she runs me ragged." He rolled his " r's " impressively. " And there's nothing in it for me. I tell you that. All I know is I miss my round of golf. I miss my bridge and I'm in trouble with Mrs. Goldfinch and her mother and all this is costing me a lot of money."

The strain of being in business and at the same time not doing any was obviously too much for Mr. Goldfinch. " Would you like to see the stuff? " he said, suddenly. " It's all right, I know what you're thinking," he went on, waving his cigar deprecatingly. " We're not likely to get in one another's way. You see we do a very high-class trade."

I followed him into the sitting-room. I had never seen so many dresses in my life. There were hundreds of them all jammed together on rails—cotton dresses, rayon dresses, silk dresses—all in fearful colours.

A tall girl with red hair and a neck like a giraffe's was sit-ting on a sofa with her legs tucked under her. Without make-up she was a dreadful sight. Nevertheless I found her more agreeable to look at than Mr. Wilkins, of whom I was beginning to tire. In a corner Mr. Goldfinch had rigged up a small portable bar on which stood a number of bottles. As he switched on the light it too lit up, illuminating a slogan "Try My Sweetie-Pie!"

"This is Polly," said Mr. Goldfinch. "Mr. Newby, a friend of mine in the business."

Polly glared at me.

"I want to show Mr. Newby some of our things," he said.

"Well, no one's stopping you," said Polly.

"I told you," said Mr. Goldfinch, hissing in my ear confidentially, "you see what a little bitch it is."

He gave me a cigarette marked "Sweetie-Pie".

"Now this," he said, taking a cotton dress from the rail, "has been Big. We've sold this very Big. McIntyre's had a hundred and fifty and repeated." It was a topless cotton sundress overprinted with a tasteful design of liqueur labels: Parfait Amour, Crème de Cacao and so on. At this hour of the morning the effect was disagreeable.

"I call it Chin-Chin," said Mr. Goldfinch.

"Who buys them at this time of the Year? Isn't it too cold for this sort of thing?"

"I don't know who buys them," said Mr. Goldfinch a trifle brusquely. "How should I know who buys them. All I know is the cotton season's practically over in January.

"This is a lovely number. Look at this one." This one had a little bolero. It was an ingenious garment. Front and back the design was the same. It represented the Empire State Building. By removing the bolero the wearer also took off the observation platform and the top twenty floors.

"The Way to the Stars," said Mr. Goldfinch, lovingly.

Both dresses looked a little woebegone. Perhaps the tremendous weight of the collection had crushed the life out of them. Mr. Goldfinch sensed what I was thinking.

"Of course they're better seen on," he said.

"They get a bit tired on a journey," I said, trying to be sympathetic.

"Listen," said Mr. Goldfinch. "If you'd been on as many women as these dresses you'd be tired."

To my surprise later in the morning Mr. Wilkins proposed that we should go out.

"A breath of fresh air, Mr. Eric," he said. "We might go for a ride on a tram. It will work up a thirst. I went once before on a Sunday to a place called Rucken Glen. A beauty spot."

We set off on a tram, swaying through streets that were utterly deserted. Mr. Wilkins smoked his pipe in silence. After an interminable journey we arrived in an outer suburb.

"Rucken Glen," said the conductress. "All change!"

Solemnly we disembarked and waited in the rain until it was time for the tram to return to the city.

At midday the hotel lounge was filled with commercials like ourselves marooned in Glasgow for the week-end, all gazing into nothingness. The only woman was Mr. Goldfinch's Polly, who hid herself resolutely behind a magazine. Nevertheless the atmosphere grew heavy with lust. There was no draught beer, presumably it was not considered a sufficiently genteel drink for a hotel, and soon the tables were littered with empty bottles. It was like being in the second-class smoking room of the Titanic. At any moment I expected someone to start singing "For those in peril on the sea."

In the afternoon Mr. Wilkins had a nap and I read a letter that had been sent on to me from Edinburgh. It was from my father.

"Do not be cast down by your experience with Miss

Reekie," he wrote. "At heart she is a good woman, but good women are sent to try us." He also counselled me against what he described as "Mean night adventures in the streets." Looking out of the window it was impossible to imagine having any kind of adventure at all unless dressed in oilskins and gum boots.

After a hearty tea Mr. Wilkins proposed another trip to Rucken Glen. It was a measure of my demoralisation that I saw nothing extraordinary in his suggestion. It seemed as good a place as any other and I went with him. That night we took the train to Manchester. By this time Mr. Wilkins had almost succeeded in driving me insane.

CHAPTER SEVENTEEN

ON THE BEACH

"YOU LOOK a bit peaky," my father said. "Why don't you go off with Wanda for a few days?"

It was December and miserable weather. I was not the only one who was "peaky". Wanda was expecting a baby in January. She was like a vast balloon filled with hydrogen and equally dangerous. Bus conductors turned green when she tried to board their vehicles. In London we lived on the fourth floor of a block of flats. There was no lift and no coal. It seemed a sensible idea.

"Dungeness is the place," said a man we met at a party that night. He was a copywriter from J. Walter Thompson, with horn rims. "It's desperately eerie. I stayed there for a week with my friend. We adored it. The people are very strange. It's out of this world." He went on to speak of the roaring fires they had made with driftwood they had picked up on the beach. It sounded splendid. He was about to give us the address of this copywriter's home-from-home when our hostess took him away to introduce him to someone else, at the same time deftly substituting a monoglot Finn with braided hair and pimples who remained with us for the rest of the evening. We never saw him again.

Dungeness in December was out of this world alright. The wind howled over the shingle and among the dilapidated wooden buildings. At the water's edge gulls fought savagely over something nasty thrown up by the sea. Eastward of the point tankers whistled mournfully as they came in close to take a Thames pilot. In the open there was not a soul to be seen. The inhabitants all seemed to have gone to earth for the winter.

We found accommodation with suspicious ease in a disused railway carriage close to the east lighthouse, one of a pair high on the shingle, at the extraordinary rental of four shillings and sixpence a day. Although in our hearts we knew that there must be something seriously wrong with the railway carriage, at such a price it seemed worth the risk.

Forewarned, we had brought with us our own bedding and a Primus Stove. The water supply was some way off but, as Wanda pointed out, "In my country you wouldn't expect running water in a third-class carriage."

"You won't be lonely," the woman in the shop who gave us the key said. "The other carriage is occupied too. Sisters. Quite elderly they are. Still it's nice to have company. And I'll give you the telephone number of the doctor. Just in case."

That night we visited a pub. It was one of those bleak modern buildings with a huge, empty parking lot in front of it that was capable of holding a fleet of motor coaches. The bar was equally empty. It was not one of those places that the copywriter had described to us ecstatically as being full of local colour. Dejectedly, we bought a bottle of rum and left. Outside it was fearfully dark. I reversed the car and there was a rending crash. With a car park as big as an airfield at his disposal someone had left his machine nose-to-tail behind our own.

It turned out to be a large lorry loaded with shingle. The lorry was undamaged but the whole of the back of our motor-car was squashed flat; worst of all petrol was trickling from the tank. The lorry driver was still asleep inside the cab of his vehicle.

At this point he woke and put his head out of the window. There was an orgy of mutual recrimination followed by an exchange of addresses. As there were no witnesses both sides were able to draw freely on their imaginations. I was angry because it was my fault for not looking where I was going and the lorry driver was angry because he had no business to be anywhere near Dungeness and had only come there in order to take a load of shingle which he was going to sell elsewhere. When, after a long wait, a mechanic arrived his verdict on the mishap was the same as mine.

"You've got a hole in your tank," he said after regarding the piece of rag with which we had plugged the hole for some minutes.

"Brilliant!" said Wanda who was making rapid strides with the idiom.

"Can't mend it here," he went on, disregarding her. Have to send it to Folkestone. Get it back Tuesday if there aren't any power cuts. Best I can promise."

It was Wednesday. We were marooned at Dungeness.

For two days and nights the wind blew force nine from the south-west. By day, bent by the wind, soaked to the skin by driving rain, yet exhilarated, we crept along the shore combing the shingle for treasure thrown up by the storm. We found hatch covers, rope fenders, the husks of coco-nuts, empty tins that had once contained metal polish or curry powder, a German mine and dozens of unexploded shells and mortar bombs, but no pieces-of-eight, messages in bottles or church plate from the wreckage of the Armada; nothing that would make our fortune and no wood dry enough to start the roaring blaze that we had been promised in South Kensington. The only fire that I managed to initiate required the best part of a pint of paraffin to get it going and then smoked like a funeral pyre in the rainy season.

By night, huddled sleepless in a bed that would have been inadequate for two people of normal proportions we listened with awe to the storm as it howled about our meagre habitation, which was by no means watertight. Soon the floors of the various compartments were littered with cooking-pots and old tin cans into which the rain dripped mournfully. Once or twice we saw a light in the other carriage, but it only flickered for a moment and then went out. Of the sisters themselves there was no sign. On Saturday evening the wind fell away completely. The rain ceased. Inland a wall of fog rose over the marsh and began rolling seawards towards the point.

"I vonder what that man is doing?" said Wanda. She was looking towards the lighthouse from the kitchen window, a non-smoking compartment. One of the keepers was unlocking a door in the side of the white building which supported the light turret.

It was just growing dark. Although the man left the door open when he went into it, it was impossible to see what was inside it in the failing light. There was the sound of a motor running for a moment, then the man came out and locked the door.

At eleven o'clock that night the carriage rocked as though it had been straddled by a broadside. Huddling on our coats we went outside, expecting some spectacular disaster. But there was nothing to be seen. Everything was enveloped in thick fog. Except for a dull glow from the carriage next door we were in utter darkness. Then it happened again. RRRRRR . . . OOG. It was more than a mere noise. It was a violent physical sensation, like being hit between the eyes.

Twin apparitions in the fog materialised as a pair of elderly ladies in red dressing-gowns with their hair in curlers—our neighbours.

"Good evening," I said. It was all I had time for before I received another blow between the eyes.

"It's the 'orn," said the taller of the two, despairingly. "Now the fog's come down it may go on for days. One short. Then a long one. Then a short."

RRRRRR . . . OOG went the 'orn as if to confirm what she said.

"It's terrible," said the other one. "You must think us unneighbourly not having called before, but we've been getting some sleep while the weather was fine. We shan't get any now until the fog lifts."

I shuddered. In the fine weather of the last three days the lifeboat had been out twice and a bungalow had been swept away by the sea.

The lighthouse keeper, used to conducting holidaymakers over his spotless domain was more informative when we approached him the following morning. Although he said it was not usual in winter time he offered to show us the apparatus.

"This here instrument," he said affectionately patting the foghorn which resembled a pair of enormous ear trumpets, "is a Diaphone, 'Twin G'." RRRRR . . . OOG roared the diaphone in its hateful voice.

Although the keeper's lips continued to move it was some moments before we were able to distinguish what he was saying.

". . . and is a most powerful instrument," he went on. "It has a range of about six miles. But with favourable conditions its range is considerably greater. It emits three blasts every two minutes. One short—one long—one short." (As if living next door to it we didn't know.) "It is unwise to stand in front of the instrument while it is functioning as this may lead to permanent injury of the ear-drums. Thank you very much, Sir, Madam! Very kind of you." RRRRRR . . . OOG.

By Monday morning we were at the end of our tethers. There was no question of sleeping. We simply waited for the thing to go off. Lying down one had the sensation of being kicked in the stomach—the effect on my wife can only be imagined. Sitting up the blast brought on a splitting headache of the sort usually reserved for sufferers from sinusitis. If the noise had stopped for even five minutes we should have both fallen asleep and not woken again. The two-minute interval was too short.

On Monday afternoon we took a bus into Rye and tried to take a room in the town but without success. Everywhere it was the closed season. Beds not already occupied, we were told, were too damp for occupation. At the best hotel the manageress thought we required a bedroom in the middle of the afternoon for immoral purposes. It was difficult to see how she had reached this conclusion.

"She must be blind," said Wanda, as we stood once more in the street listening to the mocking sound of the diaphone as it came to us across ten and a half miles of marsh, sand and shingle.

Another night of horror. At ten o'clock on Tuesday morning the fog lifted. Our motor-car was returned to us. We paid our dues; took leave of the two sisters and set off in brilliant sunshine to have a good sleep on some sand dunes near Camber that a local fisherman had recommended to us as being "nice and quiet." After the shingle in which we had wallowed for days the sand dunes were like heaven. We found a hollow out of the wind and lay down to sleep for the first time for five nights. Through half-closed eyes I could see great banks of cumulus moving majestically across a cold blue sky. In the hollow the sun was very warm.

"DER DER DER DER DER. You're dead!" said a voice. For a moment I really thought we were. Standing over us on the rim of the hollow was an extraordinary figure—a young man of about twenty with a thin beard, dressed in a khaki shirt and corduroy trousers. On his head he wore a forage cap decorated with fronds of laurel. He was pointing a piece of curiously shaped drift-wood at us that was obviously intended to be a sub-machine gun. Although he looked a lunatic, he was as surprised as we were. "I'm ever so sorry," he said, "I thought you were my friend." He made as if to go.

I was both fascinated and frightened. "What on earth are you doing?" I said.

"Well, you see," he said, "we're playing at Dunkirk. I've got my tommy-gun and my barrack 'at all camouflaged"—he pointed at the extraordinary confection on his head—"and we're playing at Dunkirk. My friend's a Jerry, not really of course," he explained, "and we're stalking one another, going DER DER DER DER DER.

"It is like Dunkirk, isn't it?" he asked, appealingly. "I expect you were there. Makes me look a bit silly, doesn't it?"

The only dunes I had seen were on the day I had made my ignominious journey to the Belgian coast when we had been stoned by the population who were under the impression that we were German prisoners.

"I don't think it's silly at all," I said. "It's just like Dunkirk." "Do you really think so?" he said, eagerly. "I looked at all the photos before we came. I want it to be right. We came down specially."

"The only thing is," I said, "I don't think you'd wear laurel leaves in your hat if you were fighting a rearguard action on a sand dune."

"You're right," he said with enthusiasm. "Those are the sort of details I miss. Not having been in it. I picked those leaves on the way down.

"Did you see that film ' All quiet on the Western Front'? " he went on, forgetting about the laurels. "That was a smashing film. Do you know the part I liked the best? The part with the machine guns. Where they were all advancing and you saw the men working the machine guns, DER DER DER DER DER DER. They killed 'em in thousands but they still kept on coming. I liked that," he said. "It was smashing. But war's awful, isn't it?

"Well," he said reluctantly, "I'd better be getting on, otherwise my friend will be wondering what's happened to me." He disappeared, but not for long.

"Sorry to trouble you again," he said, "but I don't often get a chance to talk to an expert. Do you think I could put seaweed in my barrack 'at? That would be better than laurel, wouldn't it? "

"I shouldn't bother to put anything at all. It's the man who's quickest on the trigger in this sort of fighting," I said. "Seaweed won't do you much good."

"Thanks ever so much," he said. In the distance we heard the sound of DER DER DER DER DER.*

"I've had enough of the seaside," Wanda said. "I want to go home."

More dead than alive we returned to London.

---

* Although at the time we regarded him as an object of derision, our friend who went DER DER DER DER showed remarkable prescience. It was not until more than ten years later that a film company used the dunes at Camber for the filming of an expensive epic entitled " The Sands of Dunkirk ".

CHAPTER EIGHTEEN

A NIGHT AT QUEEN CHARLOTTE'S

IN THE early hours of the sixteenth of January Wanda began to show unmistakable signs that the baby was on the way, but it was only after a good deal of argument that she allowed me to send for an ambulance.

"I don't vont to stay in those places longer than I have to," she said as I assembled the meagre collection of belongings that expectant mothers are permitted to take with them on these occasions.

The ambulance men were not unkindly, but used to more spectacular casualties, they were, I thought, more off-hand than the circumstances warranted. Nevertheless one of them remained in the back of the vehicle during the journey to the hospital and kept our spirits up with stories of accidents that had particularly taken his fancy in the course of his work.

"That was another tricky one," he said with gusto after having told a particularly gruesome anecdote about a customer who had been impaled on an iron fence. "You see the bloke had been working on a wall, demolition of bomb damage it was, and he must have knocked out the wrong brick because the whole lot fell on him. When we got there all we could see was his boots sticking out. I've never seen anything like it. Do you know . . ." He then recounted the details of what it was he had never seen anything like.

"There was another bloke who fell in a concrete mixer. . . ." And to me, "Are you feeling all right?"

I asked him if we might have the window open.

"I can see you're the sensitive sort," he said.

My wife who has an instinct for horror was delighted by these reminiscences. Perhaps they took her mind off her own pains which were now recurring with great regularity. I was less happy. Ever since I was small I had always had a tendency to faint when anyone spoke of mutilations and operations. As a grown man I had fainted during performances of "Oedipus Rex", "Titus Andronicus" and most impressively during the showing of the film "Carnet de Bal", at the point when a drug fiend has an epileptic fit in a garret in Marseilles. On that occasion I struck my head on the iron door of the emergency exit with such violence that it opened and I ended up in the street with passers-by daintily lifting their feet to step over me. I was revived by two elderly usherettes in black who saw me leave the building in this unusual fashion.

"What happened?" they said when I came-to.

I said that I had suddenly felt ill.

"I expect it was the War," one of them said, sympathetically, I thought.

"I expect it was," I said. Anything was better than argument.

"Well, you're not the only one who was in the War," said her companion.

"No, you're not," said the one who had suggested it in the first place, suddenly siding with her. "He's not the only one, is he?"

I chose this moment to go off again, but as I did so I heard them saying: "No, he's not. Is he? He's not the only one . . . the only one . . . the only one."

To make sure that I had not been mistaken I went to see "Carnet de Bal" a second time and fainted again at precisely the same moment but in a less conspicuous part of the theatre.

It was not therefore surprising that when we at last arrived at the hospital I was not feeling my best.

Although it was long after midnight Queen Charlotte's was ablaze with lights.

"It looks like a factory," said Wanda, joking bravely. To me it looked like a transatlantic liner going down with all its lights on.

"Take him back for you when you're safe inside," said the ambulance man, who seemed to have taken a fancy to Wanda. "I could tell him a lot more funny things I've seen, only he looks a bit green."

I said I preferred to walk.

"Well, just give us a ring any time you need us," he said. "That's what we're here for."

Inside the building there was an air of purposeful activity. It was very clean and very modern and very hot. We were directed to one of the upper floors where they took Wanda away. Soon she was back dressed as if for a sacrifice in a sort of cotton shift.

"Don't worry," she said. "I'm all right." And went into various minutae of domestic detail about boilers and laundry. I wasn't listening. Then she was gone for good.

I was told that I would have to take her clothes away. Whilst I was waiting for them a woman passed in front of me dressed in one of the cotton shifts. She was very, very large and her face was green. By now everything was green. Then I thought I heard screams. I tried to open a window but before I could do so I measured my length on the floor, hitting my head a tremendous crack.

"Will you be all right?" said one of the nurses sometime

later when I once more stood in the entrance hall. "We've
tried to get you a taxi but there's no reply from the rank. The
fresh air will do you good. There's nothing to worry about.
We never lose a mother and we never lose a baby."

"I'll be all right," I said. I had Wanda's clothes on my arm
wrapped up in a piece of newspaper. In the state I was in they
seemed like her "effects". "I shouldn't telephone before
eight," she said.

I set off through deserted streets. On the way I met a policeman. He was standing in the doorway of a shop.

"What have you got in that package? " he demanded.

I told him.

"Where's your wife? "

"In Queen Charlotte's."

"And where are you going? "

"Over the river. We live by Hammersmith Bridge."

"Well, go over it and not into it," he said and resumed his
vigil.

There was no news at eight o'clock when I telephoned. A
brisk female voice said that Mrs. Newby was still in the
labour ward and was "comfortable".

She was "comfortable" when I telephoned at ten o'clock,
at midday and at two-hourly intervals throughout the day. To
me they seemed to have a strange conception of comfort at
Queen Charlotte's. I was in a state of despair. I had no appetite
for food. At such a time the idea of drinking was unseemly,
like a bad joke about expectant mothers on one of Mr.
Wilkins' postcards. I roamed the streets with a pocket full of
pennies for the telephone, unable to settle anywhere. Because
Wanda was a Catholic I went into the church in Farm Street,
lit a candle and tried to pray because it seemed to me that a
Catholic church must be more efficacious when praying for
Catholics.

That night the female voice on the telephone was replaced by that of a night porter. He seemed to offer more hope.

"Listen," I said, "you must tell me what's happening. She's been nineteen hours in the labour ward and all they tell me is that she's comfortable."

"Well, you see," he said, "they're comfortable in a manner of speaking. You can't say they're uncomfortable. It wouldn't be right. Besides, you'd only be worried."

"DAMMIT, I AM WORRIED. I WANT TO KNOW WHAT'S HAPPENING."

"Ah," he said. "You want to know what's happening. That's a different thing altogether, knowing what's happening. Were you in the war? Well, you know as well as I do it's no good asking anyone what's happening in a war. It's the same here. It's like a battle, nobody knows what the hell's going on until it's over; and if they do they won't tell you. Look, tell you what, I'll telephone you as soon as it's happened —whatever the time."

That evening at my invitation a great friend of mine moved into the flat. The idea was that he should keep my spirits up. He was a man of gargantuan appetite and at midnight he produced a gargantuan meal of greasy chops served up with mounds of cabbage. It was a repast for which at any time I would have been unprepared. We dined in bed as it was very cold weather. Tony finished my helping as well as his own.

"Must keep our strength up," he said, like a family physician prescribing chicken essence for an elderly patient.

Between us we drank a bottle and a half of burgundy and fell into a coma.

At half past one in the morning I was woken by the telephone. "Hallo," said a voice. It was so distant that it sounded as though it came from the bottom of a well. "Is that Mr. Newby? It's me. Queen Charlotte's. It's all right, I'm happy to say. It's been born. Mrs. Newby's comfortable. That means she's all right."

"What's been born?"

"Half a mo, let me check."

I could hear him mumbling down a list of new arrivals.

"It's a daughter. Is that what you wanted?"

"I don't mind as long as it's a baby. Thank you very much."

"Just like the old war, isn't it? You'll get the other details in the morning. Ring 'em up about eight."

I woke Tony. Sitting up in bed we drank a bottle of champagne. It didn't blend well with the chops. In the midst of more conventional toasts we drank to Queen Charlotte's. At that moment I would have endowed it with a new wing.

The next morning whilst I was telephoning to find out what had really happened Tony brought me breakfast in bed, a week's ration of bacon and fried bread swimming in fat.

"I didn't think you'd want more of those chops and vegetables so I finished them off. One must keep one's strength up at a time like this," he said.

CHAPTER NINETEEN

A MAN CALLED CHRISTIAN

" The Season's sensation is the new house of
Christian Dior, about whom more in our
next issue."

British Vogue. March 1947

" Ankles—which glimpsed beneath the hem
of a skirt once drove the mashers to distrac-
tion—ankles are regaining their old magical
quality."

Harper's Bazaar. May 1947

MADAM HAVET, perched on her throne in the Place
Vendôme, had been right. Fashion was on the move. In
Paris in the Spring of 1947 Dessés and Fath both showed
thickly pleated skirts that were heavily padded with cambric.
There were barrel skirts, wrap skirts, jackets with standaway
collars, and boleros. In this melting pot Dior lobbed his collection like a bomb. When it exploded the line was crystall-
lized. What happened that day in the Avenue Montaigne is
history.

The Dior collection marked the re-birth of Women as they
had always existed in the minds of Men—provocative,
ostensibly helpless and made for love. He immobilised them
in exquisite dresses which contained between fifteen and
twenty-five yards of material; dresses with tiny sashed waists
in black broadcloth, tussore and silk taffeta, each with a built-
in corset which was itself a deeply disturbing work of art. By
day, superb beneath huge hats that resembled elegant mush-
rooms, they were unable to run; by night they needed help

when entering a taxi. As these divine visions moved their underskirts gave out a rustling sound that was indescribably sweet to the ear. Sometimes they wore tight little jackets with padded peplums which in the course of the next two years were to be multiplied throughout the civilised world.

But not yet. Although the Press and a few of the more sophisticated Buyers who actually saw the collection were enthusiastic the London Wholesalers received the news of what had happened across the Channel with scepticism and plain derision. It was thought to be absurd, another outbreak of madness on the part of the French, a last despairing death kick by Paris which was no longer to be the centre of the fashion world. Half-throttled by clothes rationing and frightened by the storm of conflicting emotions which Dior's collection had released, most manufacturers played for safety and made for the Autumn what they had been making for the last seven years with a slightly longer skirt.

Lane and Newby was no exception. It would be convenient fifteen years later to say that I was the one person to recognise that a truly international fashion had at last arrived. If I did so it would not be true. Although I was pleasurably excited by what had happened I did not believe that the New Look had come to stay.

Our Spring Collection was received by the Buyers in a rather languid fashion and I was thankful that my father had been able to cut down the orders for material. Nevertheless it was decided, unwisely, that we should make up the balance of what we had bought in certain proved models and sell them from stock. It is nearly always fatal to attempt to use up materials which have not sold in this way.

With this mass of innocuous-looking stock I set off on a round trip of the Midlands and the North.

It was soon apparent to me that things were not as they

should have been in the Spring of the Year. Wherever I went in every department store I was shown rail after rail of dresses, coats and suits which were not selling, and the stockrooms were packed with them.

"Can't give them away," said Miss Bellwether at Liverpool, one of the most phlegmatic buyers in the business, pointing at the glass cases in which our own productions and other dresses of the better sort hung forlornly waiting for customers who had so far failed to arrive. "They just won't buy. They all say they're waiting to see which way the wind blows. You can hardly blame them. That Dior should be shot. It's all very well for the French. They don't have rationing. All my customers are asking for is this New Look. It makes you wonder who won the War."

I was reluctant to be drawn into a discussion of this kind.

"I've got some very nice silk dresses in larger sizes, Miss Bellwether," I said. "Seven and a half guineas." They were dresses which normally sold for nine. "Ninety-nine and six," she said promptly. "And then, I'll have to put them on a special rail. To tell you the truth I'd rather not have them at all."

I did not accept Miss Bellwether's offer but quite soon I wished I had. Everywhere I went with my outmoded dresses their reception was the same. In despair I telephoned to London.

The news there was not good. According to my mother even Mr. Wilkins had been shaken out of his habitual calm by the reception he had been given at the London Stores. There was an interval while she consulted my father.

"No one is buying," she said. "Your father says the best thing is to get as much as you can for them and let them go. I must say I agree with him. If you wait much longer you won't get rid of them at all."

I immediately telephoned Miss Bellwether at Liverpool and told her that I was prepared to sell the dresses to her for five and a half guineas, providing that she bought them all.

"Of course we shan't be able to repeat them at that price." I said.

"I don't want them at five and a half guineas," Miss Bellwether said.

I waited as long as I dared before replying.

"I think we would be prepared to let you have them for five guineas."

"Too much. Couldn't move them at that. I told you," she said. She was beginning to sound impatient.

"Ninety-nine and six."

"I'll take the lot at seventy-nine and six but I don't really want them at all. It's only because I've known your parents for so many years." For a moment I thought of trying somewhere else but a terrible vision arose of another Buyer making an even lower offer. The market seemed to be collapsing fast.

"All right, Miss Bellwether." I said.

"'ERE!" said Miss Gatling when I returned to London. "That Miss Bellwether's taken her full discount on that special line you sold her. You should have told her that you were selling them nett."

"Of course I told her," I said. "I put it on the order."

"Well, she hasn't put it on her confirmation." said Miss Gatling.

Dior's second collection was shown in August, 1947. It was even more successful than the first. All the normal protuberances were given prominence but fortunately not all at once. In the jargon of the trade, breasts, bottoms and bellies were "in" which meant that in actual fact they were sticking out. It was a confusing business.

Skirts were as little as eight inches from the ground. Dark colours predominated and greys were very popular. Most beautiful were the five o'clock dresses, a time of day which in England one usually associates with nursery teas, crumpets and Gentlemens' Relish. They were of stiff black silk or chiffon. The décolletages were cut as deep as a crevasse. Below the waist they were rounded, showing to advantage what became known as *la derrière de Paris*. These dresses had an air of illicit romance. In London their inflammatory qualities were speedily recognised by the expensive street-walkers of Curzon Street and Bond Street and apart from a few grandes dames and a handful of model girls they were the only citizens seen abroad in the new fashion.

Coats had mink collars, belted waists and rounded hips; or else they were huge tents. The shoemaker, Perugia made buttoned boots for the afternoon. They were certainly not intended for playing football.

The London Couture showed skirts that were twelve and fourteen inches from the ground. Tent coats were in and for the first time the shoulders of suits were smaller. Most of the wholesale were still making the same square cut, swing-back coats and tunic dresses with square shoulders that they had been making for the last five years.

To combat them the glossy magazines gave instructions to their readers, most of whom were in difficulties because of clothes rationing, on how to convert their clothes to the New Look. They make macabre reading today. "Have a hip yoke of the same material as your skirt or wear your old jacket with a new, contrasting, longer skirt."

And because evening skirts were getting shorter as day

dresses became longer. "Cut off the bottom of your full-skirted evening dresses."

By the Spring of 1948 the London Couture Houses had all given up the long suit jacket. By April wholesale versions of the New Look were in all the shops.

Paris itself was already far ahead. This Spring fashion reached the highest point of romantic feeling. Roses nestled in bosoms, high collars were edged with lace, waistlines rose. The long winter was over. Fashion was itself again.

CHAPTER TWENTY

BIRTH OF AN EXPLORER

I SPENT THE next seven years tottering up the backstairs of stores with armfuls of samples or stock which I was anxious to get rid of. For hours and sometimes days I waited with my feet sinking deeper and deeper into the carpet for Buyers who had just gone on holiday, were just going, were in London, Paris, Berlin, Stockholm, Rome, Zurich or the ladies' powder room; had a cold, had been dismissed or had not yet been appointed; were having coffee, an affair with the Managing Director, a baby (so rare an excuse that even I was satisfied); had not yet started to buy, had finished buying, had over-bought; didn't want anything until after the Budget, Christmas, Easter, The Funeral (in the better end of the trade the decease of Royalty was always unseasonable); thought the clothes too expensive, too old-fashioned, too smart for the provinces or just didn't like them. Hemmed in by subterfuge I almost grew to love the one's who didn't like them and said so. It is not a business renowned for candour. I called on the Buyer of one London Store for five years without seeing anything but her feet protruding from under a screen.

Wherever I went in England, Ireland, Scotland or Wales I was dogged by the wicker baskets which I inherited from Mr. Wilkins when he gave up travelling. At least twice a day, I packed and unpacked them, standing waist-deep in tissue paper. Although I counted them incessantly, like a warder with a working party, sometimes one would go missing, temporarily, perhaps because by nature I was less careful than

Mr. Wilkins. On two occasions they vanished completely. Standing on the platform at York, having just alighted from the London train I saw them stacked in the guard's van of an express that was steaming out of the station bound for the south. Another time I saw them all sink into the Mersey when the hook came off the crane that was loading them into the Irish Packet. I was delighted, business was difficult, I was selling stock and the contents were adequately insured.

To reach my customers, besides trains and ships, I used motor-cars, taxis, buses and once, during a strike which paralysed the entire island, a bicycle. Air travel was normally too expensive with such a weight of luggage but once I went to Belfast by plane five days after having had my appendix out and conducted my business propped up against the wall of a stockroom in the Grand Central Hotel. Like Mr. Wilkins before me I too reached Inverness only to find that it was an early-closing day. I also spent Shrove Tuesday, 1949, marooned in Scarborough because for some unfathomable reason the inhabitants were all on the beach having a tug-of-war.

Fortunately for me, however absurd it may seem in retrospect, I had a private dream to sustain me.

One of the defects of character that I shared with my father was that I had a receptive air which encouraged other people to share with me their secret aspirations. The results of this were not always happy. In 1941 whilst I was in Tobruk a rather elderly Naval Commander approached me with the suggestion that I should test out the prototype of an infernal machine which he had invented—a torpedo that required a human being to guide it to its target which was to be the seven-thousand ton Italian cruiser, *Raimondo Montecuccoli*. The snag so far as I was concerned was that the apparatus was constructed in such a manner that its detonation required the operator to go up with it. When I showed reluctance to take part in this experiment and suggested that he should do it himself the Commander was affronted. He pointed out that if he allowed himself to be blown up with the prototype there would be no one left to construct an improved model. There was a certain truth embodied in what he said which has since gained universal acceptance amongst men of science. He never spoke to me again.

In prison I had consorted with numbers of amateur explorers: Himalayan mountaineers; men who had spent months on end in airless South American forests (one had contracted a loathsome disease in the Matto Grosso which made him yearn to eat earth); Frenchmen who had burrowed deep into the Sahara in Citroen motor-cars; and others, mostly officers of the Indian Army who had spent their leaves before the war travelling, generally without official blessing, in High Asia.

Talking with them about the wind-swept places they had visited was an agreeable form of escapism from the confined circumstances in which we found ourselves. In this cloud-cuckoo atmosphere extravagant plans were laid for vast journeys which we were to carry out together when we were finally liberated. I found myself being invited to cross Sinkiang in the opposite direction to that taken by Peter Fleming; to set off in search of a curious tribe who were reputed to live in nests in trees somewhere in the East; and to join a semi-private army called the Tochi Scouts which spent its peacetime existence skirmishing vigorously on the North-West Frontier of India.

It is a measure of my eccentricity that when I returned from Germany one of the first things I did was to prepare myself carefully for the sort of Buchanesque existence I had imagined in prison, and which I expected to begin as soon as I had "found my feet"

I ordered a formidable pair of boots from a firm that had been making the same sort of article at the time when Whymper climbed the Matterhorn. In fact, I first saw their advertisement in Murray's Guide to Switzerland, 1878, and was agreeably surprised to find that they were still in existence.

I also expended a large number of clothing coupons on a stout knickerbocker suit made from a strong-smelling tweed, the product of a peasant industry that folded up in 1946. This together with some hairy pullovers and some stout stockings from the Outer Hebrides set me up sartorially.

Realising that it was not enough to have the proper clothes I joined a Learned Society and attended the annual dinner at which I sat between a Central European savant who spoke no English and a Rear-Admiral who turned out to be stone-deaf. I was ready for anything—but nothing happened. The men I had known in prison had returned whence they came. I felt a little hurt and very much alone.

But although this came as a shock to my pride I was determined to use up some of the excess energy and imagination I had accumulated and I took to packing my knickerbocker suit and my great boots at the bottom of one of the wicker baskets whenever I was doomed to spend the week-end away from home. So that on Friday evening if I found myself in Newcastle I used to put my baskets in the Left Luggage at the station, change into my grotesque outfit and set off for the lonely country beyond the Roman Wall.

In Glasgow I used to leave the collection hanging up in the sitting-room at the hotel. During working hours I used to hide my boots in a wicker basket and my hairy suit hung on one of the rails with the other suits in the collection as far away as possible from the things I hoped to sell. In spite of this it was actually ordered on one occasion by the owner of a small business in Galashiels who was under the impression that it formed part of the collection.

"Now that's the sort of jacket our ladies like, Mr. Newby. It's a great pity you haven't anything else like that. I should have ordered it. But you know what Galashiels is. I can only have one of a style."

Glasgow was my real stepping-off place. On Friday evenings I used to leave for the hills, returning by an early train on Monday morning covered in mire. In this way I made solitary and to me impressive excursions into the wild country about Ben Ime and Ben Vorlich; once I crossed the Moor of Rannoch in a snowstorm.

The only persons who knew anything about these journeys were Wanda and the Hall Porter at the Station Hotel. It was his job to look up the trains and work out the connections that would get me back to Glasgow on Monday morning. He regarded it as a piece of amiable lunacy, less demanding than some of the requests made to him by commercials stranded in his hotel for the week-end.

If I had to take a model girl with me on the journey these arrangements became even more complicated. I usually managed to avoid this by showing the dresses "in the hand" but with some of the more sophisticated evening dresses which I was trying to foist on the customers it was commercial suicide to show them on a hanger and I had to take a model girl. It was a depressing business; either they were the victims of long-standing engagements and were saving-up for three-piece suites or else they suffered from weak ankles. Only one insisted that she was an outdoor girl and set off to accompany me to the summit of Arthur's Seat, an eminence in the outskirts of Edinburgh, in high heels—the only shoes she had with her. She made it but although it was a remarkable tour-de-force the experiment was never repeated.

In spite of my enthusiasm, after two years I cancelled my subscription to the Learned Society. The reports in the Journal of "A New Route Through the Pamirs" or "Some Notes On A Visit To The Nomads of Central Afghanistan" had for me a mocking quality in the way of life in which I found myself. Even the tickets for the monthly lectures went unused, except as firelighters.

It was not until 1956 when Lane and Newby's as I knew it was no more that someone suggested that I should go on an expedition with him to a range of mountains called the Hindu Kush*

* See A Short Walk in The Hindu Kush.

CHAPTER TWENTY-ONE

LUNCH WITH MR. EYRE

FOR MY father the peak of the year was in July when he went up to Henley for the Regatta. At Henley he was a member of Remenham. The Remenham Club is situated just short of a mile from the start. It only really exists at the time of the Regatta, when large marquees are erected in which members and their loved ones gorge themselves on lobster and strawberries and cream. There is an excellent bar for those who have outgrown food.

If ever there was a place where the stiff upper lip was cultivated it was the Remenham Club. An Englishman needed it in the years following the war in order to support such a succession of foreign victories. There, before the installation of loud speakers which allowed members to hear what was going on elsewhere on the course, one could pass the whole week of the Regatta in a cloud-cuckoo-land of one's own creation, admittedly seeing the racing at a crucial point, yet never actually seeing a finish. In all the years my father was a member I don't believe he saw the finish of a single race.

Members and their guests sat in deck chairs behind a privet hedge or in a sort of striped gazebo which was pitched on a slight eminence, only rising from time to time in order to shout "well rowed", usually, more's the pity, to Kent School or Massachusetts, before sinking down and relapsing into a coma until the next race. Members of American crews would sometimes, provided that they had been knocked out of the racing and were allowed to eat as other men, be invited to a solid tea. With their crew-cuts, at that time still a novelty, they made a startling contrast to the members in their club caps, blazers and white trousers, like visitors from outer space which, in a sense, they were.

For very old, very respected members there was a raised seat built of teak, the gift of an elderly benefactor. Although it gave an excellent view of the course downstream to Temple Island where the start was, it was noticeable that anyone who sat on it, however robust, rarely lasted more than a few seasons.

"I'm blowed if I'll sit on it," said my father when some ancient oarsman invited him to do so. At this time, in 1947, he was seventy-three. "I'll wait a bit, until I'm old."

And by the standards of the rowing world he really was young. One of his great cronies had been W. H. Eyre. Eyre—everyone called him "Piggie"—was born in 1848 and had rowed in the Thames Crew that won the Grand Challenge Cup in 1876. He spoke a wonderful English that has gone completely out of use, the sort that people talk in novels by Surtees and *Tom Brown's Schooldays*, and he was very deaf.

"Can't hear a word the young feller's saying," he once roared in the middle of the Prince of Wales' after-dinner speech to the Thames Rowing Club.

At Henley he was a tremendous figure, wearing a black-and-white straw hat with a serrated edge like a circular saw. He used to put up at the Red Lion by Henley Bridge and was sculled about each day in a skiff as big as a Royal Daimler by a succession of oarsmen who were on a roster for instant call should he want to go down the course.

Although his appearance was pugnacious he was not so by nature, and he took a great interest in rowing men who did not belong to fashionable clubs like Thames or London.

"I see the —— Rowing Club Trustees hold a lease under

which they are bound to do all repairs which, through my own carelessness (I am not so with clients), I did not know," he wrote in a letter to my father in the Autumn of 1938 when he was ninety. "You seemed to think they were likely to wind up, but I find they pay their rent promptly every quarter, so I hope they will be able to keep on. I did know two or three of their leading men but I have quite forgotten them."

At that time, in 1938, Mr. Eyre even took an interest in my own more juvenile affairs. Hearing that I was to be apprenticed in a Finnish barque he was most disturbed.

"It surprises me," he wrote in the same letter, "that Eric wants to be a sailor, and I do strongly hope that he will reconsider it, as I am certain his Mother is *sure to miss him dreadfully;* as you will also. You say that he is to be apprenticed, but I think he would give it up unless the conditions are very far better than I can remember when I was a small boy of the voyage out to New Zealand, and two years later, when we returned in a 700 ton barque, a most stormy voyage which lasted nearly six months! We were nearly wrecked coming round Cape Horn (Southernmost tip of South America) and had to put in at the Island of St. Helena for provisions.

"I was nearly ten years old then and my brother and I used to go up the masts and out on the yards and do lots of little odd jobs for the skipper and the mates. We knew every rope in the ship and lots of 'Shanties'. The apprentice's life was a *very hard one* and the poor fellows used to get a rope's ending from our severe old skipper (a very painful operation), but I suppose there will be nothing like that on the 'Line' you mention. But he will be away continually, and subject to continual risks so, as he is your only child, I do hope that you will arrange for him to have a trial voyage before he becomes bound to serve five years, or whatever the term is.

"Talk it over with Mrs. Newby and then, both of you, do all you can with the boy. Surely if he does not like Commerce there are many occupations in which he would probably do well. You might article him in some good solicitors' firm where he would get plenty of time for rowing and all other amusements whilst serving his time—or a chartered accountants' is a good 'Trade' to learn as they are fit for all kinds of well-paid Government and other posts. As are also properly trained Engineers, either Civil or Mechanical—but you probably know as much or far more than I do about starting a clever young fellow in life.

"Forgive my bothering you with all this but I cannot help feeling very strongly that, for yours and his mother's sake, he should be kept in England."

To any reader who has managed to get this far it must be obvious that the affairs of Lane and Newby Limited were not prospering in the post-war years as they should have been. The business resembled a religious house in which the members are so old that in order to carry on the daily work of the community a whole force of lay-brothers has to be recruited to hew the wood and draw the water. If the business lasted long enough my father and mother were faced with the prospect of having to pension off more than half the staff without the assistance of a pension scheme. To me it seemed better that I should leave, but whenever I suggested doing so I was reminded that the whole thing was being kept going for my benefit. To me it seemed a dubious inheritance.

Now, on every side, new, livelier firms were springing up whose principals appreciated the importance of promoting their products by giving them brand names that were redolent of candle-light and high-living for which we were no match. Most of our customers removed our labels at any rate, substituting their own; "Made expressly for Throttle and Fumble" they proclaimed or, in some cases, more shamelessly "Made in our Own Workrooms". Whilst flattering, this was unlikely to bring our name before the public.

One of the most insurmountable problems was my father himself. Omnipresent, ever optimistic, constantly devising new schemes for clearing my nasal passages and shoring up the tottering edifice that was his business, but at the same time turning a blind eye to the retribution that overhung us like a great stalactite, which after five thousand years has been rendered dangerous by high explosive, he had two blind spots in his make-up that ultimately were to prove our undoing. Chartered Accountants and Income Tax.

After the ruinous departure of Mr. Lane my father had taken into partnership another man, who had been a member of Lane and Newby's since its inception. Unfortunately, although the new partner was morally blameless, he was far less competent than his predecessor and the business suffered even more. Eventually death had removed him too and my father was forced to turn his business into a Limited Company.

It seems probable that no one ever succeeded in explaining to my father what the formation of a Limited Liability Company entailed. I think he believed that it was a polite fiction that divested him of the onus of liability and at the same time allowed him to be a partnership without a partner.

It would be easy to lay the blame for this at the door of his accountants, but it would scarcely be just to do so. They were a firm of almost incredible rectitude. For years they had been imploring him to let off those parts of the premises that were put to no practical use. The building was held on a lease and there came a time, in the middle of the Blitz, when it would have been possible for the Company to acquire the freehold extremely cheaply. But at the time my father was seriously ill and convinced that I would never return alive and the project was allowed to lapse. It is difficult to believe that it was allowed to but it was. Overnight we acquired new landlords and things were not as they had been. The new lease was extremely short and the rent rose to an unprecedented level.

Far worse was the question of expenses and taxation. As a partnership my father's business was inextricably mixed up with his private life. If he wanted a boat varnished he had it varnished. If he wanted to go to Henley he went to Henley. He never experienced any difficulty. For years and years his business was solvent and, providing that his partner did not object, there was no one else to object.

Once Lane and Newby became Lane and Newby Limited everything was quite different—except to my father. The elderly accountant, who used to spend a week on our premises each year getting out the figures was in despair. He used to hover apprehensively in the hall for hours with a list of unacceptable expenses waiting for my father to arrive.

"Mr. Newby, I must speak to you."

"Ah, nice to see you, Perkins," my father would say genially. He had probably just returned from some eccentric errand such as the one when my mother, who had a house property in a seedy part of Pimlico, had asked him to collect the rent which had fallen into arrears. Apparently the house had become infested with whores.

"I'll get 'em out!" said my father, ferociously, and proceeded to give my mother a lecture on the folly of being soft-hearted with her tenants and her general incompetence as a Landlord. He had returned some time later without the rent, having bought the elderly mother of the three tarts a bottle of Guinness.

"She was a miserable old thing with varicose veins," he said. "There were three daughters. They all had children, all illegitimate One of them had a nasty cough. People like that have no idea how to manage their own affairs."

"Mr. Newby," Mr. Perkins would say, "I'm afraid there are certain expenses here that the Inspector is likely to query. In fact I fear that he may find them totally inadmissible. Perhaps you would be kind enough to cast your eye over them . . . For instance, this!

"Doing up bathroom in flat £20 0s. 0d. I don't think the Inspector will accept that."

"Oh," said my father, bristling as he always did when the Inspector of Taxes was mentioned. "And why not? It's my bathroom, isn't it?"

"That's just the point, Mr. Newby, it's your bathroom, not the property of the business."

"We used to have a bathroom here at 54, until the fire. Surely I'm entitled to a bathroom?"

"You can build a bathroom here at number 54 if you want to, Mr. Newby, although I imagine the Inspector would query that too; but you can't charge up your own bathroom."

"I can't see why not," my father said. "There's still only one bathroom."

The Accountant abandoned the struggle. "You want to leave it in?" he said.

"Well I'm certainly not going to pay it out of my own pocket. This fellow's just a doctrinaire, Jack-in-office," my father said.

"Then there's this item. 'Visit to Naval Review, Spithead. Fares. Train to Portsmouth and ticket on paddle steamer and return.' Mr. Newby, the Inspector will have a fit."

"We had a jolly good day," my father said indignantly. "We saw the *Vanguard*, a magnificent vessel but a complete waste of taxpayers' money. It's people like me who paid for it."

"But Mr. Newby, were the expenses incurred solely and

wholly on the Company's business? If so you can charge them as 'Visit to Portsmouth' and they will be allowable."

My father ignored this helping hand.

"Certainly not," he said. "I took the day off."

"You know," he said when the Accountant had withdrawn to his cubby hole, "these taxation people are strangling the country—cutting off its life-blood."

The financial difficulties in which the firm found itself were not of particularly recent origin. Paradoxically, only the outbreak of War had saved it from extinction. In the winter of 1937 a serious crisis arose but on that occasion it seemed that financial assistance might come from an unexpected quarter and put the business on its feet when one morning a letter arrived from Mr. Eyre inviting my father and myself to lunch with him at his club in Pall Mall. In spite of the fact that I knew that I myself was unlikely to inherit anything from anyone, on this occasion, although I was only eighteen years old, I did cherish a hope that perhaps something might be forthcoming that would at least help my father to emerge from the financial labyrinth into which he had already strayed and from which there seemed to be no visible exit; especially as Mr. Eyre's letter was couched in what, to say the least of it, were rather mysterious terms.

"I think that it is time for us to meet and have a good talk about the future," he wrote. "Although I feel in good health how long will it last if I get no more hard exercise?"

Even my mother was excited by the prospect. "He has a great admiration for your father," she said. "He is one of his oldest friends."

On the appointed day my father and I presented ourselves at Mr. Eyre's Club. "Piggie" seemed smaller than I remembered. He was dressed in a suit of antique cut (it would have been surprising if it had been otherwise) and he wore woollen mittens, but his face was the same craggy, pug-nosed affair that I had always admired and that earned him his nick-name.

"LET'S GO TO TABLE," he said in a thunderous voice that made several members turn in their tracks like London Taxis. "OTHERWISE THERE'LL BE NO VITTLES. THERE AIN'T MUCH IN ANY EVENT."

Despite his fears the lack of vittles was less apparent in the Reform than it was in the places where I was accustomed to take my lunch. There was game soup and game pie and turbot and crab and lobster and oyster and cold pheasant and roast duck and apple sauce and roast Surrey chicken and bread sauce and trifle and boiled jam roll and Stilton cheese.

Because Piggie was very deaf my father had provided me with a small block of paper and a new pencil so that I could write down any questions which I might wish to put to him in the course of the luncheon.

He himself was similarly equipped.

We ate game soup and turbot and roast chicken and jam roll and Stilton and we drank sherry and claret and port. It was a noisy affair, not because we were made hilarious by what we were drinking, but because of the difficulties of communication. Fortunately, so far as I was concerned, there was little need to say anything. Piggie and my father were far away in a deep communion over matters that had happened in another century, long before I was born, before my mother was born. It was not surprising that they more or less ignored my exist-ence. Piggie had been born in 1848, my father in 1874, in such a hierarchy I was a non-starter.

"Fellers don't train like they used," said Piggie, helping himself to a large slice of Stilton. "When I was reading the Law I lived with old Vyse in Putney—that was in '69. We were training for the Grand. We used to get up at five-thirty, walk down to the boathouse at the Feathers and go out in a heavy tub hard at it up to the Bridge and back down to the West London Railway Bridge. If it was low water we used to bathe in the river. Then breakfast, usually a chop and some stale bread. After work we used to go out again in the dark and rowed it hard down to Chelsea; then another dip in the river; then a steak and some strong ale. Then we'd do six miles on the road to harden up our legs, hard at it. We had boxing, too, three nights a week. I used to sit up three nights a week reading law until two or three in the morning. I don't recommend that. Pass the port."

My father was expanding too. At first he had made use of the scribbling pad, now, under the influence of good wine, he abandoned it.

"As soon as the shop was closed (as a young man he had been apprenticed at a shop in the Brompton Road) I used to hare off to Whitechapel. There was a feller there called Mendoza at the Six Bells."

"WHAT YE SAY?" screamed Piggie.

"MENDOZA, THE SIX BELLS."

"Yes, yes. No need to shout."

"Paid a shilling to one of the pugs for a good pummel."

"WHAT?"

"PUMMEL. Then I had a good rub down, followed it up with a pint of stock ale and a hot pie in Petticoat Lane and heeled and toed it back to the shop."

"CAN'T HEAR A WORD," said Piggie.

It took more than this to put my father off. He had told me this story on innumerable occasions.

"One morning I walked into the department, I was in piece goods, with a terrific black eye. A real shiner. The Department Manager came up to me as soon as he arrived and said,

'You must decide either to give up fisticuffs or the Drapery Trade.' As I'd been apprenticed as soon as I left school I had to give up boxing. I took up wrestling."

"Can't hear a word," said Piggie. "Help yourself to port."

"Top-hole port," my father wrote on his pad.

"Should be," wrote Piggie, "Cockburn '96. Glad you like it."

"Sorry," he said. "No need to write. Forgot you ain't deaf. Affliction of old age."

Three o'clock struck, four o'clock. The two old men went on and on. After the initial difficulties they seemed to settle down to a sort of rhythm in which one suddenly ceased to speak as if conscious that he ought to give the other a go. Occasionally, under the benign influence of Cockburn '96, both would doze off for a moment or two.

"1877. We licked the Guards Eight in the Grand. They weren't fit by half though there were some splendid athletes among 'em."

"Hippo Smith. He was a cock-up-sporty sort of chap."

"WHO?"

"HIPPO SMITH!"

"AH, yes."

"We walked together to Brighton (it was my father talking now) in '91.

"We started from Westminster Bridge just before midnight. It rained the first twenty miles. After thirty the sole came off old Hippo's boots. Fortunately he was able to buy a pair from a postman. We only stopped twice; for the boots and a hot rum and milk. On the way back in the train we got such cramp that we couldn't get out of the compartment at Victoria. It was the old South Coast Railway then. But we had a good rub down and soon we were as right as rain."

"Last year I rowed in the Grand was '82," said Piggie. "I was getting on a bit then, besides I'd had an illness."

When we emerged from the Club darkness had fallen. There had been no mention of the mysterious letter with its hints about the future. In fact there had been no mention of the future at all—or the present for that matter.

"That was a jolly good blow-out," said my father. "I enjoy a talk with old Piggie."

CHAPTER TWENTY-TWO

THE END OF LANE AND NEWBY

THE FIRM staggered on into the Fifties. Its affairs became more and more involved; its existence more and more an anachronism; the authorities more persistent in their demands for arrears of tax.

It was unfortunate for firms like ours, if any similar can be imagined, that the excess profits tax was calculated on the basis of the amount of trading that had been done in 1939, a poor year in which Lane and Newby had been on the verge of collapse anyway: anything over and above that figure was liable to tax. Companies formed after 1939 were of course not liable to this assessment. It was also possible for a company to go into voluntary liquidation and re-form itself under a different name. In this way its liability for tax became purely conjectural. It was an anomaly that only the Inland Revenue could have devised.

In spite of the disadvantages under which we laboured all would have been well if only my father had set aside sufficient money each year from his business to pay the tax when the time came but he was lulled into a false sense of security by the lack of urgency displayed by the Inland Revenue. They were in no hurry. I think, too, that he thought that by procrastinating death might remove him from the scene and with him his liabilities. Sinister-looking envelopes marked "On His Majesty's Service" continued to arrive but remained unopened.

The blow finally fell in 1953, when my father received a

registered letter ordering him to present himself at the Office of the Inspector of Taxes.

My mother was as alarmed as I was. The only person who seemed in no way put out was my father.

"I suppose I'll have to go and see the fellow," he said. "I expect his bark's worse than his bite."

"You must go with your father," my mother said. "Then at least someone will know what is going on."

At the appointed hour we arrived at the office of the Inspector. As soon as I saw him my heart sank. It was perfectly obvious that whatever was going to happen would be by the book.

My father began to chat easily about the state of the country but he was cut short.

"Mr. Newby, Lane and Newby Limited," said the official, adjusting his pince-nez and sifting through a great heap of documents. "Excess Profits tax in respect of the years . . ." He reeled them off, there seemed an awful lot of them. "We don't seem to have got very far with you Mr. Newby. The sum owing is a considerable one. You realise that no doubt. Some seventeen thousand pounds. To be precise seventeen thousand nine hundred and forty-seven pounds, sixteen shillings and fourpence. I am to inform you that unless this sum is paid within seven days we shall take legal action to recover it."

I was shattered by what he said. I had imagined a large sum of money being involved but nothing like seventeen thousand pounds payable in one lump. There was a period of silence during which I thought of Wanda and the children, that was broken only by the sound of a clock ticking on the wall behind us. It was a sad, hateful room. Apart from the clock its only decoration, which now had a particularly significant quality, was a calendar, askew on one wall.

"You realise, sir," said my father, "that if you insist on being paid all that in a week we shall be in serious difficulties."

"That Mr. Newby, is of no consequence to the Inland Revenue. If your company goes bankrupt as a result of not paying its taxes then I must point out that it will be no loss to the National Economy. We can only hope that its place will be taken by a more efficient organisation."

"That is all, Mr. Newby," he went on. "May I again remind you of the precise sum. Seventeen thousand nine hundred and forty-seven pounds, sixteen shillings and four-pence. Good day to you."

The interview was at an end. He did not bother to open the door. The next moment we were in the street.

We took a bus back to Great Marlborough Street. We didn't speak. Each was busy with his own thoughts.

"You know," said my father as we stood outside the door. "I'm afraid we shall have to consult our creditors. I'm sorry for your mother's sake. And it'll mean selling my double-sculler."

"What about the skiff?"

"You know," my father said, "if I sold it some waterman would buy it and hire it out by the hour. I wouldn't want that to happen. I'm going to try and keep it for you."

Somehow the tax was paid. How it was done I shall never know, there was no Mr. Eyre to save us, and we consulted our creditors who somewhat reluctantly allowed us to carry on.

Troubles of this kind never come singly. Our lease at Great Marlborough Street came to an end and the cost of renewal was so great that we were forced to move to smaller premises, little more than two rooms. It was a great blow to my father.

We moved house in bitter weather. Most of the furniture had to be sold or stored; the accumulation of more than fifty years was swept away in a single morning. Perhaps worst of all for my father was the loss of all his newspapers for which there was no room in Henrietta Place. His store of port, too, was much diminished and he was down to the last six and a half bottles.

My father and I stood in the hall at Great Marlborough Street and drank the last half-bottle out of tumblers. All the glasses had been wrapped in newspapers and carted away. There was no carpet on the floor, the house was an empty echoing shell. The street door was propped open as the removal men had left it and a howling draught blew through the house. Brandon was waiting outside to lock it for the last time. My father was wearing a battered tweed overcoat, a woollen comforter and mittens. He looked very old and his eyes were watering with the cold.

Nevertheless he smiled bravely.

"Jolly good wine, old thing," he said. "Fonseca, '27. We shan't see anything like this again for a bit."

He drained his glass, put it down on an upturned box and put on his hat.

"No good crying over spilled milk," he said.

Together we went out into Great Marlborough Street.

Only a skeleton staff stayed with the firm when it moved to Henrietta Place. Some of the older members had already retired, others alarmed by what was happening had gone elsewhere. I remained for a time and then left to become manager of the wholesale department of a couture house in Grosvenor Street. My father managed to save his skiff from the wreckage. In the summer of 1954 when he was over eighty he suggested that we should take it up to Henley.

Bray to Henley is about seventeen miles by water. We did it in six hours against the stream. It would have been hard work for a man twenty years younger. My mother steered, Wanda sat next to her and our two children trailed their hands in the water and were told to "sit her up" by my father. It was like old times.

It was the Friday before the Regatta, and as we toiled up past Remenham Barrier, a school crew in training came down towards us, beating it out.

"Look how they get their hands away," said my father. "They're a good lot of chaps."

Further up by Phyllis Court, opposite the enclosures, an elderly and extremely irascible friend of my father's giving his wife an airing in a similar and even more magnificent equipage, raised a hand in salute. Two small boys, each with a scull, were making heavy weather in a dinghy under the eye of a stern-looking parent who wore a pink Leander cap. At the landing stages a sculler was just setting out. He got a nod from my father and shyly raised a great fist in return. My father didn't say anything more, but when we reached the boathouse above Henley Bridge and the boatman helped him out, I knew that he was satisfied that he had brought his boat to a place where it would be appreciated at last.

He died in the winter of 1956. When I visited him for the last time in the early hours of the morning he was being given a blood transfusion. For a number of years we had shared the same wine merchant in St. James's Street. It was an arrangement that worked all right except when Berry's sent him my bills by mistake.

He looked at the bottle suspended above the bed, then he looked at me. "Wish it was a bottle of old Berry's burgundy instead of some other feller's blood," he said. "They know a thing or two about wine."

CHAPTER TWENTY-THREE

MODEL BUYER

Although the book really ends in 1956 with the death of my father three years after he had paid the astonishing sum of seventeen thousand nine hundred and forty-seven pounds, sixteen shillings and fourpence to the Inland Revenue (fifteen thousand of which he had withdrawn from the London Safe Deposit in which it had been reposing in a strong-box in neat stacks all done up with pink ribbon) it was not, unfortunately for me, the end of my life in the dress trade, a business for which, although I persisted in returning to it, I must appear to the reader to have been somewhat miscast.

I carried this money up Regent's Street for him in a Gladstone bag. We walked because it was raining and there were long queues for the buses and we didn't want to spend money on a taxi. On leaving the Deposit my father had closed the strong-box, paid the custodians what was owing for the hire of it and handed over the key. There was no point in having it any more. He would have been better advised to have gone bankrupt but it would never have occurred to him to have done such a thing; neither, strange as it may seem, did it occur to me to suggest to him that he should do so.

After this epic payment had been made I left the firm and worked for a couple of years or so at Worth Paquin, the couture house in Grosvenor Street. In my spare time I wrote my first book which I called *The Last Grain Race*. It was published in the Autumn of 1956. The events leading up to my departure from Grosvenor Street and the subsequent adventures which befell me and my companion, Hugh Carless in Nuristan, "The Country of Light", are described in *A Short Walk in the Hindu Kush*.

On my return from Nuristan in the winter of 1956 I found myself with this book to write for which I had already been given an advance and with a family to support and no money to do it with. The advance had all been consumed in making the expedition and keeping my family alive while I was away.

There is a belief, cherished by the readers of books about outlandish parts that the publishers dish out money to the writers who work for them in the same way as they pay the expenses incurred by their own employees in connection with their business. This, of course, is not true. All that a writer can hope for is an advance from the publisher which is set against any royalties which the book may earn when it is written.

In my case the only source of income which I had at that time was the royalties from *The Last Grain Race* and these were insufficient to keep us all alive, or any one of us for that matter. While working on *A Short Walk* I also wrote articles and some short stories for the *Evening Standard* but there is a limit to the number of short stories that one can write – I once produced three in a week. There was also a limit to the number of short stories which the *Evening Standard* wanted, written by an unknown hand.

It was fortunate that at this critical time my then publishers offered me a job and I worked with them until 1959 when I left to go to the John Lewis Partnership with whom I hoped to earn more money. Fortunately for us all, during these years I had been given a lot of work by *Holiday Magazine* in New York who could pay very large sums to any writer who was prepared to work hard enough for them.

The following year I became Central Buyer for the Partnership of "Model Gowns"—I was officially known as the

M.G. Buyer and I bought for about a dozen stores. This was a job which, according to the testimony of some of the previous incumbents to whom I was able to speak before taking it on, was about as safe as working in a factory engaged in making nitro-glycerine. I attributed this to the disenchantment of failure but it did seem surprising to me that the Partnership should bring in a buyer from outside it when they had so many of their own staff to choose from. But, apparently, this was a common practice.

As M.G. Buyer I had an Assistant Buyer, an efficient person who had outlasted a number of my predecessors, and a hard-working staff. I bought dresses of every conceivable and inconceivable shape and size, except short-waisted ones for which there was a special buyer. I bought day dresses, dresses with jackets, long and short evening dresses, what used to be called "cocktail dresses", and still are for all I know, bridesmaid's dresses—the most unbuyable and unwearable garments in the world—and a huge number of wedding dresses. I shall never forget the spectacle of starry-eyed girls in winter coats and plastic macs and sheepskin boots trying on wedding head-dresses on the ground floor while the snow fell outside in Oxford Street and turned to slush. Most time-consuming and boring of all was trying to buy "specials" for wives of members of the top brass.

As a buyer I was a better selector than bargainer, although I pulled off some good coups as well as perpetuating some disasters. I was not good at money but I was good at getting things to the branches when they needed them in a hurry. Sometimes I felt more like a Commander-in-Chief or a Quarter-Master-General with twelve armies operating on twelve different fronts (the branches) each of which had to be supplied with stores and munitions (dresses) at precisely the right time for them to be used in battle against skilful and ruthless adversaries (the customers).

I found that relatively little of a central buyer's time was taken up in actual buying. Most of it was spent deciding how much of the total budget for the season should be committed to buying before the season began and how much should be kept for later when one would know better what the customers wanted, by which time it was usually too late to buy it. You had to decide how much to spend on various types of dresses and how many to buy at various price levels and what size to buy and in what proportion to buy them. Should one buy very large sizes? Statistically the answer was "no". These were a few of the things a central buyer had to decide before he even set foot on a manufacturer's doorstep.

Much of my time was spent travelling between Oxford Street and Brixton, Southampton, Sheffield, Liverpool, Sloane Square, Nottingham, Holloway, Reading, Hampstead, Cambridge, Southsea and Windsor, marking down the slow-moving stock and talking to the department managers, sterling women who, having been in the wholesale myself, I felt I had known all my life. This enormous round of visits took so long that by the time it was completed it was necessary to start again.

To stop myself going mad, twice a year I used to go off to France and Italy to see the fashion collections there.

In Florence the couture and boutique collections were shown in the Sala Bianca, the great, white, rather chilly-looking ballroom in which the Kings and Queens of the House of Savoia had once cavorted. In it a seemingly endless procession of sometimes good, sometimes magnificent, sometimes completely dotty clothes passed before my eyes and those of the massed bands of international buyers and fashion journalists who sat around the catwalk noting and sketching away in their Kalamazoo and Hermès notebooks.

There were always at least fifty American buyers representing, to name a few, I. Magnin of San Francisco, Saks 5th Avenue, Ohrbach's of West 34th Street, Wanamaker's of Phil-

adelphia and Neiman-Marcus of Dallas, Texas, besides hordes
of manufacturers and designers from 7th Avenue.

Store buyers such as these had the best seats, at the T-
junction of the catwalk where the model girls turned in their
tracks like London taxis, perhaps discarding a coat or jacket to
reveal some additional surprise underneath before making the
long haul back to the changing room.

And there were great herds of German buyers in those now
far-off days giving a big hand to the mannish, the military and
anything that looked as if it had been put together with rivets;
and lots of patient, sad-looking manufacturers from Zurich,
dreaming up equally sad derivatives of what they saw in double
jersey. Apart from myself and my fellow buyers from the
Partnership the English were a meagre contingent in 1962: two
buyers from Dickins and Jones, some manufacturers from
Steinberg and Susan Small and two gloomy-looking little men
from Gor-Ray Skirts, our combined presences a tribute to
either our loyalty or our good fashion sense, in contrast to that
of the majority of English buyers who, having read somewhere
that Italy was finished because some Italian fashion houses had
moved to Paris, assumed that this was really so and stayed
away.

In 1962 for the first time there were Japanese buyers in the
Palazzo Pitti, the women in full tea-house regalia, the men in
carbon-copy black suits. "If they're going to bring the same
expertise to the garment industry that they've shown in bring-
ing everyone else's optical industries to a near standstill, we'd
better watch out", was the observation that emanated from
Mrs. Guggenheim Henry of Wanamaker's, Philadelphia when
these orientals showed their appreciation of some neat little
number. This was the first year, too, I covered the Italian
collections for the *Observer* under the pseudonym Jo Gray and
learned how difficult it is to write coherently about fashion.

I had already learned to be careful about what I bought from these high fashion collections, more careful still about what I bought and actually had copied. The previous Autumn I had bought a beautiful dress made by Roberto Capucci, one of the designers who subsequently migrated to Paris in what came to be known as *Il Volo delle Rondinelle*, The Flight of the Swallows. A very simple, slightly waisted dress, made in a beautiful, knobbly sort of bouclé wool, its principal novelty was that it was sleeveless and could be worn by night or day with equal propriety. Katharine Whitehorn, the then fashion editress of the *Observer*, was also taken with it and offered to photograph it and feature it in the paper on 27 August, providing that I could get stocks into the stores by 28 August, which was less than two weeks after I returned to England with the toile. The biggest problem was the material, which I finally found after a desperate search in an Irish nunnery where the nuns had been making it for years. It came on the market dead on time in a choice of black, cream and a very pretty pink at £16 5s 6d (£16.28p approximately) – and stayed on the hangers, even at Peter Jones, the most modish of the Partnership's stores. It continued to stick until I had marked it down to something less than £5, at which price it was bought by some of the more daring assistants. This sort of sleeveless dress subsequently became incredibly popular, and almost a uniform among the elegant blue-rinse ladies of America, and eventually it did become a uniform when some of the more chic airlines adapted it for their stewardesses. There was absolutely nothing wrong with it. My mistake had been to buy it a year too early.

Paris that Autumn of 1962 was far more hectic for a buyer than either Rome or Florence. Life in it so far as I was concerned seemed to be made up of either running from one salon to another, most of which were in the 1er or 8ème arrondissements, or else being immobilised between them in a taxi,

sometimes, but rarely, with one of the last of the Parisien White
Russians at the wheel: from Jacques Heim in Avenue Matig-
non, to Chanel in Rue Cambon, to Givenchy in Avenue
George V (but never to Balenciaga in the same street to whose
salon that great genius denied entrance to the hoi-polloi such as
myself), to Lanvin and Cardin in the Rue du Faubourg Saint
Honoré, to Dior in Avenue Montaigne where its new designer,
Marc Bohan, had been an instant success, to Saint Laurent in
Rue Spontini, in the 16th arrondissement, whose Left Bank
look was big news in 1962, to Nina Ricci in Rue des Capucines,
to Balmain and Venet in Rue François (1er). Rushing about in
this fashion, one only seemed to eat very late at night.

The French crammed their trade customers into their showrooms as tightly as they had their *poilus* into cattle trucks a few
years previously en route for Verdun; so closely shoulder-to-
shoulder that on one occasion I found myself annotating my
neighbour's programme. The heat was incredible. At the Balmain opening the temperature outside was 88° Fahrenheit
under an overcast sky. Inside, with all the windows shut,
conditions were indescribable. French vendeuses were
apparently impervious to heat. Remembering a tenuous
acquaintanceship with Mademoiselle Spanier, one of Balmain's
top people – she had a talented sister at Peter Jones – we asked
her for, and got, some Evian to see us through.

The kick-off took place with one of Bergdorf Goodman of
Fifth Avenue's buyers in the seat of honour, a homely looking
soul with a glint of steel in her eye. What followed was a real
international jet-set collection with sable lined coats dropped
contemptuously on the catwalk, sometimes exposing suits with
very long jackets with side vents, very wide shoulders and inset
sleeves with the tops where they go into the shoulders raised in
what are known in the tailoring business as rope-heads. It was
as if an old-fashioned woman dressmaker had been let loose in

a suit workroom run by a man. The skirts of these suits were either straight or very slightly flared and ended one inch below the knee. Unless a woman was tall and willowy or, failing that, elevated on the highest heels, she would look as broad as she was long. That Autumn I bought a *toile* for an evening dress from them, in thanks for the Evian, a short dress from Venet, a comparative newcomer who had been a tailor and cutter with Givenchy, whose clothes were beautifully made and cut and would date less quickly than those of many of his contemporaries, and a funereal but beautiful black chiffon from Chanel that would never date at all, the sort of dress that the Misses McAndrew with whom I had battled in Glasgow in what now seemed a lifetime ago (themselves now sunk into the tomb) had taught me to love. Black was, as Louie or Harry or Charlie, my new-found friends among the manufacturers in West One who I was trying hard to love would have said, "very, very big" in Paris that autumn, and I could almost hear them saying it as they sat in their showrooms in their beautiful dark mohair and wool suits, with their monogrammed shirts, their unscuffed shoes, their freshly manicured nails shining with clear varnish, their freshly capped teeth and their aura of male toiletries.

On the day I left the Partnership only two suppliers of the host that had besieged me during my reign wished me well, and they were the least affluent. Returning one evening to the buying office when the rest of the staff had gone home I had a revealing conversation with one of the richer ones who thought he was talking to my successor, who had not yet been appointed.

During my stewardship of M.G. Buying I received offers of weekends in yachts (but never sailing yachts), holidays in the South of France ("Mima and I are just going down to the Carlton for a few days. We would very much like you and your wife to accompany us."), offers of dinners in penthouses in St. John's Wood and outings to night clubs, offers of theatre tickets and offers of expensive objects – one of the most expensive was a crocodile bag from Hermès which I knew, because I, too had an eye for merchandise and had window-shopped in the Faubourg St. Honoré, cost something in the region of four hundred pounds. At Christmas I was offered cases of wine. One buyer was offered the childrens' school fees.

The Partnership's penalty for accepting any material offerings except for a smoked salmon sandwich and occasionally a glass of champagne, which could be regarded as a sort of viaticum, was instant dismissal. I used to accept wine at Christmas from manufacturers with whom I did business. It made not the slightest difference to what I bought from them, although neither they, nor my employers would have believed this. As one old buyer, revered within the Partnership and outside it said: "It's a wonder and a credit to us, that with a rule like this, there are any of us left at all."

In August, 1963, on a nasty, grey morning at six a.m., I arrived back from Italy where I had been attending the showings of the high fashion collections in the Palazzo Pitti in Florence to find a letter from the Chairman awaiting me, giving me the sack. My family were all abroad. No one enjoys being given the sack at dawn on an empty stomach and I was no exception.

Eventually, I went with Wanda to India and we floated down the Ganges, with another advance on royalties. Then, when I was again wondering how on earth I was going to live while writing *Slowly Down the Ganges*, I was offered the job of Travel Editor of the *Observer*. My ten years at the *Observer*, one of the few jobs I was not sacked from, were amongst the happiest I can remember.

EPILOGUE – THE LAST TIME I SAW PARIS

In January 1985, I went back to Paris with two senior editors from British *Vogue* to attend the showings of the Spring and Summer Haute Couture Collections. In doing so I was partly inspired by nostalgia, partly by a genuine enthusiasm for fashion, which in spite of the very different way of life I have pursued since abandoning it, has never been extinguished from my, I hope, still fairly manly bosom.

We put up at the Lotti, the old, rather stylish hotel preferred by *Vogue* in Rue de Castiglione between the Place Vendôme and Rue de Rivoli, in which some seventy years previously my parents had spent their honeymoon, insulated from the fury of my father's partner, the awful Mr. Lane. I had also stayed in it on the occasion when my father had sent me to consult the almost blind seer, the couturière Madame Havet, at her premises in the Place Vendôme in the Autumn of 1946 in order to confirm his own conviction about fashion being 'on the change'. At that very moment, unknown to any but his workroom staff, Dior was mixing the ingredients for the succession of bombshells which he was to launch in the Avenue Montaigne on the morning of 12 February, 1947, until that moment unseen even by his own vendeuses.

Now, in 1985, we arrived at the Lotti from Charles de Gaulle to find that the Lotti, itself one of a chain of more or less venerable hotels, had been bought by an Italian company whose hotels rejoiced in the name of Jolly Hotels and that the Lotti had become the Jolly Lotti, something that the staff did their best to conceal from us. So recently had this happened that the ashtrays, soap, book matches, toothpicks, bath towels and other such ephemera left about for the convenience of guests still bore the simple device *Hotel Lotti* and for this reason became instant collectors' items.

We were very upset. It was as if some food chain such as Wimpy had bought Maxim's and renamed it the Wimpy Maxim's. As someone said, "I mean to say you simply can't go around telling people who ask you where you're staying that you're at the Jolly Lotti. It'd be like saying you were at the 'Jolly Hockeysticks'. People would fall about."

That was Sunday night. Outside it was dam' cold. There was a perceptible air of tension in the city. General Audran, Director of International Affairs at the Ministry of Defence had been shot dead by terrorists outside his residence two days previously and the Crown Prince of Saudi Arabia was paying what might well prove to be his last visit anywhere. By Tuesday the whole of Europe was on Red Alert.

The first collection we had seats for that Sunday night was Nina Ricci's. It was to be shown in the Pavillon Gabriel, in Rue Gabriel, a street that bisects the rarefied area which has the Champs Élysées on one hand and the British and American Embassies and the Palais d'Elysée in which M. le President makes the best of a nasty job, on the other. Always a street with more gendarmes and plain clothes men in it than ordinary Parisiens, on this particular night their numbers had been increased by whole coach-loads of armed reinforcements who were now disposed along its length from the Place de la Concorde to the Rond Point.

Few, if any, of the grand couturiers held the first showings of their collections in their own salons anymore, however grand, not because there was insufficient space for their customers but because of the demands made by television and the press. Instead they hired, at God knows what cost, large halls such as the Pavillon Gabriel, or the great, glittering Salon Opéra in the Grand Hotel in Rue Auber, with its gilded caryatids supporting tiers of mirrors, or the equally astonishing Salon Impériale in the Inter-Continental on Rue de Castiglione. The latter is one of three salons in the building declared by the government, as is the Salon Opéra in the Grand Hotel, to be *monuments historiques*. Luckiest of all was the couturier Pierre Cardin who actually owned a Pavillon in Rue Gabriel in which he was able to show his seventieth collection in thirty years and his 20,000th model, rent free. In addition to other chunks of Parisian real estate he also owned Maxims and therefore didn't have to worry about where to eat after the show.

Later, when all the collections had been shown and everyone had gone home, and everything that could be written about them of any news value had either already been published or sent to the printers, I realised that that first showing of Nina Ricci, less memorable in fact because at such an early stage I had not, as it were, got my eye in, was an epitome of everything I subsequently saw in the course of the next three days and nights. Some houses showed more models. Some had more flamboyant customers. Whether one was a better or worse collection than the others was a question of taste or a matter of opinion. With such high standards, anyone who condemned a couture collection in Paris in January 1985 in its entirety was a fool.

Above the catwalk a maze of currently modish, high-tech girders supported the lights that would soon pour down on it and the photographers of both sexes who crouched on either side of them. Some were Japanese using German Leicas; everyone else used Japanese Nikons. Up there, under the lights, it was terribly hot and some of the photographers wore beat-up old safari jackets that could have done with a visit to a laundrette. Others wore sleeveless vests, displaying, when they raised their cameras, expanses of armpit that made me feel a bit off-colour on an empty stomach. Some took long, lingering looks at the distinguished guests who were mostly also distinguished customers through their 150mm lenses. One was reading a newspaper piece headed *Accusé D'Avoir Tué Un Travesti Pour L'Amour D'Une Femme On Avait Retrouvé Découpé Dans Le Bois De Vincennes*, which didn't make me feel so good either. Facing one another across the catwalk were the rows of seats which, when the showings used to take place in the couturiers own salons, would have been occupied by the big-store buyers, now booked solid for the world's press, about ninety-five per cent of them women in all shapes, sizes and colours, all now currently engaged in talking away to one another nineteen to the dozen. The only one who wasn't sitting with them was Hebe Dorsey of *International Herald Tribune*, doyenne of Parisian fashion journalists, who always occupied one of the *places d'honneur* at the head of the catwalk where she sat amongst the customers. Because of this, like some ungrizzled courtier, she knew almost as much about the private lives of those she sat with as she did about fashion, which was why the arrival of the Herald Tribune under one's bedroom door was an eagerly awaited event. The only big, international store buyer she identified as being present at these showings was Sonja Caprini of I. Magnin, San Francisco who admitted that she liked them better than the ready-to-wear, which presumably meant she was going to buy some of them. "Sit there," said Liz to me, indicating a little gilt chair with a card on it which read VOGUE G.B. MADEMOISELLE BEATRIX MILLER. "What, *me*?" I said. After all, Miss Miller was Editor of Vogue G.B. and had been since 1964. I felt unworthy to occupy her seat. "Yes, *you*," she said. "She hasn't arrived yet. Maybe she won't come at all this time." So I did, feeling like Walter Mitty on Olympus, more or less the only man within sight among an awful lot of girls.

Then all at once, when it seemed that the Ricci faction had lost interest in starting the proceedings, some unidentifiable signal was flown, the lights came on, the plastic sheet intended to keep the white catwalk free from the hoof marks of people like me who take size twelves was whisked away, the men with the armpits picked up their cameras, adjusting their fully thyristorised dedicated flashes, or whatever they were, and to the strains of what was in this instance celestial music, equally otherworldly model girls came streaming up the runway. Taller than real girls even in their socks, they were now wearing stiletto heels, eight centimetres taller than that, and slimmer than anything you ever meet in real life. Girls of every sort of colour: the white of the drifted snows of the Caucasus, the palest of sangue melées, the malarial yellow of the extrême-orient and the deep black of the jungle. Girls so ungirllike that you could forget that they were girls and concentrate on what they were wearing – as well as one could with the photographers' flashes flashing brighter than a thousand suns – which was what I knew was intended.

And what would the customers be wearing after ordering from Nina Ricci? Amongst other wonders they would be cloaked in long, broad-shouldered jackets with inset belts in houndstooth checks, teamed with long, contrasting houndstooth pants, draped blouses in black and white striped satin silk with black and white turbans to match – the sort of outfit that Garbo might have worn for a meeting with Barrymore in *Grand Hotel*; headgear impossible to buy unless you've bought the rest of the outfit, and although very swish, a tiny bit vulgar. And there were dresses in lots of spotted silks, in yellow and fuschia, and black and white, and écru and rose, in mousseline and crêpe de Chine; there were satin sheaths with straps that appeared to be embroidered with precious stones and one beautifully draped, embroidered orange satin number with an orange stole, that received some applause. Here, at Ricci, there were none of the transports that greeted some of the outfits shown by Yves Saint Laurent, or Ungaro, or Chanel, later in the week.

What were they for? Where could they be worn, these and other clothes I subsequently saw? For yet more shopping, probably in the Place Vendôme; for travelling in Rolls Royces fitted with purdah glass to deter the curious from looking in; for holidays in yachts that never weigh anchor; for the sort of people who, someone himself rich (was it Onassis?) is reputed to have said, have no need for overcoats.

What do they cost, these garments? No one who hasn't bought one, or doesn't know someone who has, sufficiently well to ask them, really seems to know. A consensus of not necessarily well-informed opinion suggests that that simple *tailleur* might begin around 30,000 francs (say £3,000), rising through to 60,000, 100,000, or even 150,000 francs for a grand evening dress, at the time of writing in the region of £15,000.

How can such prices be justified? In terms of time and materials consumed dresses of this sort must be almost as difficult to cost as, for example, a definitive model of a sailing ship, of which the maker can never hope to recoup in money what he has put into its construction in terms of man hours. In time alone a great evening suit or dress can consume between eighty-five and 100 hours in the making, not counting the time it took the designer to first create it in his imagination and then put it on paper, plus sixteen hours to sew ribbons round a big skirt. In the Autumn of 1976 British *Vogue* photographed a collection of evening dresses made by

Lanvin, Saint Laurent, Ricci, Ungaro, Givenchy and so on, of really exceptional beauty. One of these, by Jean-Louis Scherrer, was a floor-length black taffeta tent-shaped dress embellished with a wide band of gold braid and emerald embroidery, and to be worn over it, an equally long, all-enveloping taffeta cape with a high shawl collar. The dress took ninety-two hours to complete, the cape sixty hours and the embroidery, which was only a deep band, ninety-seven hours. And there are dresses that can swallow up twenty-five metres of satin and embroideries.

For anyone brought up in Britain it is difficult to realise what the Couture means to France. When, on the Monday morning following the Sunday evening showings of the first two of the twenty-four fashion houses, *Le Figaro* ran a front page which read '*Triomphe . . . leur heure de gloire . . . un moment prestigieux . . .*" they were not referring to some such moment as when General Galliéni saved Paris and saved France in 1914 by sending taxis loaded with soldiers to hold the line on the Marne. They were simply rejoicing in the fact that a M. Mouclier, Président of the French Chambre Syndicale had announced that the couture business for 1984 had totalled 270,000,000 francs an increase on 1983 of thirty-five per cent. This was the week, too, in which Saint Laurent, after a triumphal show, announced that with an after tax profit of $5,000,000 last year, which derived from everything from boutiques to cigarettes bearing his name (but not the perfumes which belong ultimately to Squibb Pharmaceuticals) he was going to turn his business into a public company and offer his shares on the Bourse.

And who wears these clothes? Women as different as Madame Valéry Giscard d'Estang, Paloma Picasso and Sylvie Varton. Dior alone has 500 faithful clients.

With uncountable thousands dying in the Third World,

with millions unemployed in Europe, should such extravagances be permitted? But it is not only an industry, it is an art form and one that employs thousands, many of them women. Dior alone employs 130 seamstresses. The Couture also supports a great textile industry.

The workers are not rich, but if by some mad decree they were dispersed, their skills would vanish from the face of the earth. I still remember the girls in our own model workroom, high up in our house in Great Marlborough Street with its big glass window overlooking the rooftops in which the light cast no shadow and the quiet, withdrawn expressions that they wore, expressions of an incommunicable satisfaction.